MYSELF AND MICHAEL INNES
A Memoir

MYSELF AND MICHAEL INNES

A Memoir

by

J. I. M. STEWART

LONDON
VICTOR GOLLANCZ LTD
1987

First published in Great Britain 1987
by Victor Gollancz Ltd,
14 Henrietta Street, London WC2E 8QJ

British Library Cataloguing in Publication Data
Stewart, J. I. M.
Myself and Michael Innes.
1. Stewart, J.I.M.—Biography   2. Authors,
English—20th century—Biography
3. Critics—Great Britain—Biography
I. Title
823'.912   PR6037.T466Z/

ISBN 0-575-04104-8

Typeset at The Spartan Press Ltd,
Lymington, Hants
and printed in Great Britain by
St Edmundsbury Press Ltd,
Bury St Edmunds, Suffolk
Illustrations originated and printed by
Thomas Campone, Southampton

Contents

Acknowledgement

Parts of the Oxford chapter originally appeared in *My Oxford* edited by Ann Thwaite and published by Robson Books.

List of Illustrations

CHILDHOOD

Some Pictures

ON EITHER SIDE of our grandfather clock, and flanked to left and right by stags' heads impressively antlered and with a faint smell, hung two large pastel portraits, identically framed and very much designed each to chime with the other. On the left was my great-uncle John Innes Mackintosh, a physician in Hull later resident at Caistor in Lincolnshire, my only kinsman known to have been a foxhunting man. As I glance at him in passing now he shows as florid and robust, with abundant dark locks lightly curled and reddish Dundreary whiskers, but in his fortieth year already perhaps a shade too heavy in the saddle. The portrait is a good one, and the artist has signed and dated it: Anthony de Salomé, 1859. The companion portrait — surely to the perplexity of any of our visitors who reflected on the matter — is of a lady attired in mid-eighteenth-century costume, with a white rose in her hair. She is not, as she might conceivably be, my great-aunt in fancy dress. The lady of the rose is Anne Mackintosh, familiarly known as 'Colonel Anne', and Salomé's portrait is a copy of one by Allan Ramsay the younger. For Dr Mackintosh, instead of commissioning a companion portrait of his wife, despatched the artist to Moy Hall to take at second-hand the likeness of this celebrated heroine. My great-uncle was, so far as I know, unrelated to the owner of the Allan Ramsay except in the obscure but often emotionally potent sense of membership of a clan. I myself have sufficient of this in me to create a certain interest in Colonel Anne's story.

During the '45 the then Mackintosh of Mackintosh, like many of his kind, prudently declared his loyalty to the King. Less prudently, he actually had himself commissioned in the Hanoverian forces and took the field with them. He was promptly captured, and by the Chevalier de St George courteously returned to Moy to remain in the custody of his wife, who had meanwhile brought out the clan in the Chevalier's interest. She is said to have rewarded with a kiss every man who took up arms, and quite certainly she achieved the trick that came to be known as the Rout of Moy. Lord Loudoun, commanding 1,500 government troops at Inverness, heard that Charles Edward was spending the night at Moy, and advanced against the mansion with — very foolishly — his entire force. Anne Mackintosh, forewarned as was inevitable where such a large movement was concerned, charged Donald Fraser, the Moy blacksmith, and four other men to delay Loudoun's nocturnal advance through the Pass of Moy. The ruse succeeded beyond all rational expectation. Firing their guns and shouting stentorian commands to imaginary Mackintoshes, the five men caused the entire enemy to bolt in disarray. It is sad that Walter Scott was unable to enlist this celebrated panic in the first of the Waverley novels.

Unfortunately my pastel portrait of Anne Mackintosh is in poor condition, having at some time been unskilfully 'cleaned' in an Edinburgh picture shop. Any informed person would at once say, 'That's after Allan Ramsay', but now the shepherd who stands behind St Joseph in Piero's Nativity in the National Gallery is in much the same condition as poor Colonel Anne. There is even the suggestion of an *écorchée* about her, or at least of a lady who has been kept under trying conditions for a long time before being wheeled out on a tumbril. Something like this briefly threatened Colonel Anne after Culloden. She was conducted to Inverness in circumstances of marked indignity, and before being returned to Moy had to hear talk, facetious rather than ferocious though it probably was, of being hanged with a silken cord from a mahogany gallows.

I have the impression — although it may be a mistaken inference from the bungled clean up — of Salomé's crayons being called upon to achieve their effect boldly or against time. Perhaps it bored him to have to reproduce in pastel another man's oils. Or perhaps he had been received without much cordiality at Moy by a Mackintosh apprised of the quasi-conjugal status which the copy was to be accorded in Hull by a member of his clan whose existence had probably been unknown to him.

With some slight eccentricity, my great-uncle appears to have called his Caistor house Εἰρήνη, since it is the address that his widow appends, in Greek characters, to a note on the back of his portrait bequeathing both portraits to her sister-in-law, Mrs Dunbar. This lady, my great-aunt Marianne Mackintosh, born

in 1832, was probably regarded as the most socially exalted of
the eleven children of my great-grandfather by his wife,
Margaret Innes Simpson. She had married Lewis Dunbar, a
younger son of a Moray baronet with a respectable seat near
Nairn called Boath House. As a boy, Lewis had gained family
celebrity through swimming out to the island that gives its
name to Loch-an-Eilean, then one of the last nesting-places of
the osprey in Scotland until the bird's recolonization in the
middle of the present century. My father supposed that young
Lewis was 'after the eggs', but in this he may have been
attributing to his uncle activities of his own in Forres a generation later. Lewis eventually became a distinguished ornithologist. Two engravings, of innumerable land fowl and sea fowl
respectively, given to him by the artist, J. G. Millais, a son of
the Pre-Raphaelite painter by Ruskin's unfortunate former wife,
have come down to me in much better condition than has the
portrait of Anne Mackintosh.

It seems that in early childhood I was accustomed to regard
Salomé's efforts as representing Miss Cook and Miss Richardson. Whether such misconceptions can really accompany the
dawn of life, I don't at all know. It is possible that I was
conscious of achieving a stroke of humour. The actual Miss
Cook and Miss Richardson were among our nearest neighbours, living in a semi-detached house two along from our own
in the village (as it then was) of Corstorphine outside Edinburgh. I can see now that Miss Cook must have come down in
the world. What early struck me as mysteriously significant was
Miss Richardson's calling Miss Cook Miss Cook, whereas Miss
Cook called Miss Richardson Richardson. I am, of course,
writing about the first decade of the twentieth century, when
maiden ladies of even very modest means might employ a
'companion' as well as a servant or two. When I now summon
up a picture of Miss Cook's drawing-room I see Miss Richardson scurrying round with cushions, fire-screens and footstools.
This may be a piece of embroidery rather than a true recollection. More certainly authentic is a glimpse of myself perched on
Miss Cook's sofa and suddenly wetting it — this because I had
failed to obey an injunction to 'make myself comfortable' before
going with my mother to pay an afternoon call on the two
ladies.

It is curious that an occasion so impolite should harbour among my earliest memories, and I search for more refined recollections. Those afternoon calls were an important part of our village life. My mother had little pasteboards, to be left on other ladies' hall tables, bearing some such information as 'First and third Thursdays' by way of guarantee that on these dates her board would be spread and her housemaid properly dressed. The drawing-room bell-pull would also have to be in order, since a high impropriety would attend any guest's departing without the little maid's having been summoned to 'see her out'. I imagine that Miss Cook's possession of Miss Richardson assured her of a more or less exalted station in this society. But she was not right at the top, since in Corstorphine there was also a certain Lady Nicholl, whose deceased husband was mysteriously described as having been an Indian Civilian. I remember nothing of Lady Nicholl herself, but can quite clearly hear the respectful tone of voice adopted by all her acquaintance when her name fell to be uttered.

What other pictures were there in my parents' house in addition to Miss Cook and Miss Richardson, and the engravings of land fowl and sea fowl by J. G. Millais? There was a sampler — which I still possess — of Lot escaping the fate of Sodom and Gomorrah. He sits on the ground with his knees clasped within his arms, and although his head is turned in the direction of the doomed cities he is looking cannily straight up to heaven. His wife has not yet become a pillar of salt — something it would have been difficult to represent with any degree of artistic success — but her gesture is despairing and she clearly knows what she is in for. One of the patriarch's two daughters is represented as still a young child, and is thus the more easily fitted into what is a rather sophisticated pyramidal composition. Presumably the ladies who executed the pious scene had some work by a professional artist to go on. It is odd to think of them thus labouring at a prelude to incestuous high jinks in a cave above Zoar.

There were other religious pictures, including several large steel engravings of Raphael's cartoons for the Vatican tapestries. These were splendid things. One, that of Peter and John healing the lame man at the Beautiful Gate, was perhaps the first work of art to command my imagination. I pored equally over the hideously mutilated creature supporting himself on a staff to the right, and the incredibly lovely woman with the basket on her head and the child with his thank-offering of doves beside her which balances the composition on the left.

Quite a different kind of picture became important to me round about my ninth year. We had a stereoscope. The *Oxford English Dictionary* quotes somebody as recording in 1863 that 'the stereoscope has now become a drawing-room toy', and I suppose ours was that. It was an extremely simple optical instrument which presented as a single three-dimensional image two pictures of an object respectively taken from a minutely different point of view. One slipped into a frame an oblong of cardboard showing side by side two dull and null little photographs of an identical scene. Then one viewed this through a lens to an effect that was wholly magical. The picture had taken on body and substance before one's eyes. It was as if one could walk about in it!

Some of the scenes thus available to me were merely soppy: doting gentlemen and languishing ladies making eyes at one another in what appeared to be florists' shops. But there was a whole set of pictures — certainly as many as fifty — depicting activities in the Boer War. I was already entranced by these when in our household's random collection of books I came upon a chronicle of the war by one of the Boer generals, Christian de Wet. It is the first book I can remember reading again and again — and certainly with the stereoscope beside me. The narrative, although not notably partisan, was written from the Boer point of view; the stereoscopic photographs had nearly all been taken from within, or behind, the British lines — if lines there were. Something potentially educative, I suppose, inhered in my being thus poised between two sides of a conflict.

I believe there was no education at all in another sort of pictures: the 'pictures' to which one 'went' in picture houses, picture palaces, picturedromes, cinemas and kinemas. Ten years later, indeed, and by the time I reached Oxford, many films had become ecstatically funny (whether inadvertently or by design) or deeply moving — but this was perhaps in part a consequence of their being shown to audiences whose ages would have averaged out at twenty. As a juvenile addict in Edinburgh (and I was a considerable one) I got, so far as I can remember, nothing out of these pictures except a certain numbness — and why I was driven to seek this means of dissociation is obscure to me. What I chiefly recall of such occasions is the unfortunate woman who in the near darkness played the piano. It was before the age of those monstrous organs that used to rise up out of the bowels of cinemas to assault the ear between films. With (I suppose) occasional exhausted pauses, the lady tinkled away throughout the session, making little if any attempt to match her music to the spirit of the representation on the screen. Her effort was indispensable, all the same, since the jerky knockabout comedies and violent serial melodramas would have been intolerable if transacting themselves in an unnatural and grisly silence.

It was far otherwise with the offering of Mr Poole, with which I must have become acquainted some years before beginning those solitary hauntings of cinemas. The *O.E.D.* (once more a never-failing fount of knowledge) quotes the *Scotsman* as recording that in Edinburgh in 1901 'Mr C. W. Poole . . . opened a short season's engagement with his myrioramic entertainment'. It also quotes the *Westminster Gazette* as informing an English public that the Edinburgh School Board (of which my father was the principal officer) had paid for the admission of 2,000 children to this instructive diversion.

A myriorama is, or was, an elaborated form of panorama — the word then used to describe a vast picture so disposed upon revolving cylinders as to afford spectators the sensation of surveying an extended scene. Mr Poole's myriorama did better than this. It contrived simultaneous movement on several planes, different speeds and opposed directions. And the lighting effects were very up-to-date.

Mr Poole showed me the sinking of the *Titanic*. The disaster occurred on 15 April 1912, and as Mr Poole's had become an annual Christmas-season event in Edinburgh I must already, by the age of six, have heard much, and taken in a little, of the catastrophe. And here, suddenly, it was. Mr Poole, conscious, it may be, of the confidence habitually reposed in him by the Edinburgh School Board, was a stickler for historical accuracy. On the forefront of his stage he could, when he wished, do you a sea storm worthy to prelude *The Tempest*. Nothing of the sort now. The curtain goes up on a tranquil Atlantic shimmering beneath brilliant stars, and with a gentle swell to it barely perceptible as one looks. There is a clear horizon line — not so

Young John with his mother

Father

John aged eight

The Edinburgh Academy

JIMS with his mother
1921

Driving parents round
England 1924

lacking in curvature as to give schoolchildren the misleading impression that the world is flat. On what might be called the backdrop floats a single thin drifting cloud. For some seconds the cloud obscures first the head and then the tail of the Plough. So we are gazing north.

It follows, too, that the doomed liner must appear on our right. We wait for it, already in agonizing suspense. Its bow appears — just. In fact it is pausing a shade hesitantly in the wings. It advances again, a blaze of minute lights near where sky meets ocean. A faint music is heard: *The Blue Danube.* As is proper on this vast floating luxury hotel, there is revelry by night. We look left, knowing what we are about to see. And here it comes! Ever so slowly, the iceberg is drifting east. It is like an enormous twirl of confectioner's sugar on top of a cake, but faintly green and therefore hugely sinister. These two objects duly collide. There is a dreadful sound — I don't know how contrived — of impregnable steel punctured and ripped open as might be a tin of sardines. One small boy is momentarily conscious of nothing but a hideous clutching in his reins. The iceberg disengages itself and glides smoothly (or almost smoothly) on. Most of the lights on the *Titanic* have been extinguished. The *Titanic* tilts slowly and then slowly disappears — stern first or bow first: I don't remember — beneath that peaceful ocean.

Nor do I remember whether, in those last moments, we heard the strains of the liner's orchestra playing *Nearer my God to Thee.* . . . If we did, it wasn't a matter of Mr Poole's a little yielding to sensation and piling it on. That the orchestra did think thus to encourage the hundreds of passengers desperately struggling to get into the liner's numerous but hopelessly skewed and tangled boats was for long almost universally believed in as both plausible and edifying.

Joseph Conrad wrote two tremendous denunciations of what he was convinced was the intolerable degradation of seamanship constituted by the ruthless commercial development of such opulent monstrosities as the *Titanic.* Thomas Hardy, in a famous poem, set the catastrophe within a time scale beyond Mr Poole's scope:

> And as the smart ship grew
> In stature, grace, and hue,
> In shadowy silent distance grew the Iceberg too.

In a sense, I suppose, the *Titanic* disaster was swiftly eclipsed by the ultimate horror (as we then conceived it to be) of the First World War. But I must be only one among many Edinburgh contemporaries who, mute before Mr Poole's spectacle, are haunted by it still. Certainly as details came to me later — the *Californian* only eight or ten miles away, but its wireless operator in bed; the distress rockets seen from the same ship, but ignored — I felt a growing sense of bewilderment before the human situation. And some fifty years on, while returning from New York on an American cargo boat (called, I think, the *American Trapper*) in extremely bad weather, and being summoned to the bridge by the captain in the middle of the night to admire the flag-ship of his line, a vast liner in a blaze of light overtaking us on the horizon, I found myself thoroughly frightened. It wasn't, oddly, for myself (although in my cabin my cabin-trunk was hurtling itself against the ship's plates in what I judged to be a highly undesirable manner) but for the smoothly and swiftly gliding vessel which would reach Cherbourg long before us. I knew there couldn't be any icebergs around. But what about some other lurking hazard: an old drifting mine, or a submerged hulk, an uncharted rock? These irrational fears went back to the myriorama of Mr C. W. Poole.

To this account of a large-scale entertainment I may add, as a kind of footnote, mention of a very small one which I recently came upon in a drawer. It dates from the early days of cinematic photography. The camera has been focused on a single brief action; the resulting frames have been stacked in due order like a pack of small patience-cards and firmly bound together at the base; when rapidly flicked over at the top the result is a kind of Lilliputian movie. My father and a convivial friend (I recall his name; it is the Reverend William Main) are sitting side by side with tankards on a table before them. They pick up the tankards, elevate them in the manner of men toasting one another, drink largely, set down the tankards and exchange satisfied nods. It is like the briefest of advertisements on commercial TV. But here has been my father alive again. He died in 1946.

And now I am prompted to search my memory for my first acquaintance with the talkies. It was certainly after my schooldays, and perhaps when I was an undergraduate with, among other things, the experience of the great Russian silent films behind me. But I associate the occasion still with one of Mr Poole's ventures in Edinburgh's Synod Hall. (This may be a confusion.) As I face the screen it is as if I am looking straight down a garden path. A figure appears at the end of the path and silently advances towards the audience, including myself. Amazingly, he turns out to be the then current god of my idolatry! He comes to a halt before us, apparently as surprised as we are at the encounter. But at once, and most courteously, he addresses us. 'Ladies and gentlemen,' Bernard Shaw says, 'good afternoon.' And the era of the talkies has begun.

SCHOOL AND UNIVERSITY

Scottish School

EDINBURGH HAS A number of boys' schools of ancient foundation. George Heriot, the 'Jingling Geordie' of *The Fortunes of
Nigel*, who was both jeweller and banker to James VI, founded a
'Hospital' for the support and education of fatherless sons of
indigent freemen of the city, and this school flourishes today. So,
too, do both George Watson's College, the creation of a banker
who died in 1723, and Daniel Stewart's College, founded at the
beginning of the nineteenth century by a Scot of humble origin
who had made a fortune in the Indies. But historically more
distinguished than any of these is the High School, older by
several centuries than the others, and at the close of the eighteenth
century still beyond question the greatest of Scottish schools.
William Drummond of Hawthornden was educated there, and so
were James Boswell and Walter Scott, as well as most of the
literary and legal luminaries who dominated Edinburgh society
in the period during which the city liked to think of itself as the
Modern Athens.

About the High School, however, a slightly later generation of
former pupils was increasingly critical. Henry Cockburn recalled
that during his many years at the school there had not been ten
days on which he had escaped flogging at least once, but on the
whole he was more disturbed by the dreariness and inefficiency
distinguishing the manner in which classes of up to a hundred
boys had come to be dragged through a classical curriculum. 'We
were kept,' he wrote, 'about nine years at two dead languages
which we did not learn.' And of these there was far too much
Latin and far too little Greek. Everybody knew that, in this
particular, Eton was streets ahead of Edinburgh's High School.

Yet the cardinal fact about the High School was that it
remained, in the now popular and useful sense of the word,
democratic — as, indeed, for centuries, were broad areas of
Scottish education as a whole. Gentle and simple sat on the same
forms, studied the same aridly-presented subjects through the

23

same weary hours, were beaten with the same vigour. There was also much undisciplined rough and tumble, and in the fights and brawls that regularly took place elements of class antagonism were certainly at play. It was so, too, in the *bickers* indulged in by the juvenile populace in the streets of the Old Town: battles with stones and sticks and fisticuffs in which — Lockhart tells us in his *Life of Scott* — 'it happened that the children of the higher classes were often pitted against those of the lower'. So when, with the astonishing building of the New Town, the 'higher classes' removed themselves across the Nor' Loch to territory exclusively their own, the idea started up that the New Town should have its own new Edinburgh Academy. Lord Cockburn himself was the prime mover here. It would be greatly to the advantage of the scholars living in the new district to be relieved of the need for a twice-daily trudge through insalubrious and at times disorderly regions in order to maintain their studies at the High School, still located in what were already thought of as the slums.

There was a great battle over this, admirably described by Magnus Magnusson in his history of the new school, *The Clacken and the Slate*. One result of the conflict was the municipality's removing the High School to a site midway between Old Town and New, and erecting for the purpose one of the finest classical buildings in Scotland. But the new school won through, being opened on 1 October 1824 by the prematurely ageing author of *Waverley* himself. Magnusson is obliged to reflect that 'the Edinburgh Academy, from its birth, reflected a degree of social or class orientation, and . . . did represent the first major break with the democratic traditions of Scottish education.'

There was a good deal of family debate about my own schooling. My mother's only brother, Jimmy Clark, had been at boarding school — whether to his advantage or not it was impossible to say, since he had died young. My father's schooling had been extremely simple. The Edinburgh High School had by this time joined those 'Board' schools controlled by a publicly elected authority of which my father was the executive officer. I am quite sure that I should have made a very indifferent High School boy, but the possibility of my going there was not considered, since my father felt that some awkwardness might result from such an arrangement. His own choice would probably have been George Watson's, the principal grammar school (to employ the English term) of the city. But this was an issue upon which my mother carried the day. I entered the Edinburgh Academy hard upon my seventh birthday, and left it — abruptly but entirely of my own volition — eleven years and a week later.

The Academy was still something of a citadel of Edinburgh's *haute bourgeoisie*, and particularly of those professional people who were connected with the lairdly classes. My mother must have found this state of affairs important, since I recall her taking me aside and urging me to remember that the Clarks were a sept of the Frasers. I had no idea what this meant, and it almost certainly meant little, but the information was intended to help me keep my end up among exalted companions. My mother, who was nothing if not romantic, would have been happy to believe me descended from that Simon Fraser, Lord Lovat, who was the last man to be beheaded on Tower Hill for high treason. I possess to this day, as a consequence of the characteristic Scottish concern with 'connections' whether real or imagined, a formidable volume printed in 1747 which records *verbatim* the entire proceedings at the impeachment of Simon Fraser in Westminster Hall.

Duncan Pattullo, the narrator in my sequence of five novels, *A Staircase in Surrey*, devotes a number of pages to describing his schooldays at what is plainly the Edinburgh Academy. They are at least glancingly autobiographical, and I remember them as having been written fairly easily. This may have been because — so far as the school went — there didn't seem to be much in my head from which to disengage them. My memories of my schooldays are scanty and unremarkable, yet they cover eleven years! On more than two thousand occasions, that is to say, I must have pushed my bicycle into those pebbled yards in the morning, and then out of them in the afternoon, whether homeward or to some playing-field. I don't doubt that in that long stretch there was plenty of fun, as well as much boredom and a certain chronic apprehensiveness never amounting to anything like terror. Every now and then, the school having broken up (or 'skailed', as my father would have said), we were treated to the spectacle of some peccant wretch waiting, perhaps in rain or snow, before a door through which he would presently be summoned for the purpose of being whacked on the bottom by half a dozen of the beefiest boys in the school. The muscular giants were called *ephors* (our Spartan word for prefects) and their weapon was a *clacken*, which was like a monstrous wooden spoon with a flat surface, normally used in a kind of primitive hockey-cum-lacrosse known as *hailes*, and inherited from the High School. Every now and then, too, and in the presence of their fellows, boys would be mercilessly flogged with a *tawse* by such of the masters as liked that sort of thing. (This never happened to me except in a comparatively mild and ritual way: I think it was the beefy giants-to-be that chiefly afforded satisfaction to their mentors in this regard.) I recall, on the other hand, very little bullying. The 'boarders' ran to a good many tough characters of whom one had to be wary, but the day-boys at that date outnumbered them by — I suppose — about three or four to one.

Yet if I didn't find school particularly alarming I did find it rather dull, and I believe that this was only partly my own fault. As not in the Academy today (in which, as in most similar 'independent' schools, there is every sort of going-on under the sun), nothing much that could be called 'extra-curricular' occurred; and the subjects studied were presented for the most part in a dry and unimaginative way: this because there was supposed to be virtue in intellectual effort purged of anything other than intellectual effort for its own sake. I 'did' Latin for most of those eleven years, but I had to go to Shakespeare — and to Oxford — before discovering that there had once been Romans. Except for 'English' — rather a soft subject — I was a thoroughly mediocre pupil throughout the greater part of my time at the Academy. This had the disabling effect of largely cutting me off from the clever boys of the school, although I was reasonably clever in my own way.

I don't think that this lack of a particular kind of social intercourse worried me other than quite obscurely. I got along very happily on the basis of a single close friend at a time: first, and rather briefly, with a boy called Mervyn; and then with Jim, who became my sheet-anchor for years. Jim was to study medicine, and I believe he became a reliable G. P. He was much better at games than I was, but not greatly interested in them. We mucked and pottered around together, and were in and out of each other's home, without cease. This close companionship was different from occasional perplexing obsessions with good-looking and attractively rebel younger boys. With one of these, Harry Watt, I was all-mysteriously thus obsessed for months.

When I left school Harry dropped out of my life. A long time was to pass before I learnt that Harry, who had directed in Australia a famous film called *The Overlanders*, was to have directed for MGM what proved to be an abortive film of *The Journeying Boy*, to my mind the best of the Michael Innes stories. Harry died a good many years ago.

The Academy masters, although a varied crowd, exhibited one common feature. They were nearly all English and Oxonians, and therefore spoke a dialect with which the Directors of the school presumably judged it advantageous that we should become acquainted. I found these noises attractive, and somehow consonant with the Anglican prayer-book the contents of which figured with an odd prominence in our morning devotions. It is my impression that after the day's work the masters tended to retire into a world of their own, and I can't recall any of them figuring in my life outside the boundaries of the school. But I liked them and got on with them very well. The only exception was a Mr Green.

George Buckland Green taught at the Academy for 34 years, and may well have been — although I don't actually know — senior classics master throughout that period. Certainly, and unlike most of his colleagues, he was very distinctly a scholar, and responsible for sending on to Oxford a succession of boys some of whom became eminent scholars in due time. He was also an ambitious but rather worse than indifferent cricketer, and we believed that his having come to Scotland (which he vastly disliked) had been in the hope of shining on cricket-fields less exigent than those south of the border. But in addition to presiding over an awesome egg-head eminence known as the Classical Seventh he had the bread-and-butter task of acting as form-master of a bunch of middle-school mediocrities called 5B. In 5B I spent a bad year under Buckie Green. He was an acrid and obstinate elderly man, and never rid himself of some initial impression that I was in 5B in furtherance of a life of ease gained through a brash and culpable masquerade. That a boy could be reasonably intelligent and at the same time a hopelessly inept fabricator of Latin proses and unseens was a notion which, whether rightly or wrongly, he totally rejected, and he would regularly inform me in class that my prizes for one or another frippery ought to be taken away from a boy academically so reprobate as I daily proved myself to be. I am still in possession of a photograph of Mr Green, apparently clipped from an Edinburgh newspaper and on a mount adequate for the reception of the signatures of everybody in 5B, declaring itself to be an award for my having received from Mr Green a number of *poenae* constituting a record for the school.

A day came in which I found myself in the Classical Seventh! This seems to have been because the Academy at that time had a very scanty organization on the modern side, and didn't know how otherwise to accommodate a boy supposed to be aiming at a history scholarship. That morning — the first morning of a new term — I must have known it wasn't going to work. But at first this came to me as a confused dislike of my new class-room. Particularly, I didn't like its pictures. There was one of what is called the Farnese Hercules. There was another depicting captives being ritually scourged as they passed beneath a yoke and thus exchanged freedom for slavery. It was when thus discontented that I was addressed by Buckie Green. 'Well, Stewart,' he said with extravagant grimness, 'I never expected to find *you* here.' I can see now that this was designed as an accommodating remark; signalled an intention of *rapprochement*. But what it triggered off in me was the realization that, a few days before, I had attained my eighteenth birthday. I was grown up, with 5B far behind me. It was time to do a little thinking. So for the rest of that morning — and while my class-mates of the moment were, I suppose, planning their term's assault on sundry Greek and Latin texts — I did manage something in the nature of clear-headed calculation. I much doubted (I judge correctly) my ability to win a history scholarship at Oxford, particularly from a school like the Academy, which my present comical situation showed as at an academic level Classical rather than Modern through and through. Moreover I believed (accurately, I think, in 1924) that if I did win such a scholarship it would oblige me to read for the History School, whereas I wanted to read English. All this was clear to me by the time the dinner-break arrived, and I then left the Classical Seventh class-room along with my companions — but with the difference (I have come to believe) that I made Buckie Green a slight bow. I then walked out through the gates of the Academy, and I have never been through them since.

I had behaved very badly, and everybody else behaved well. The school's headmaster — known as the Rector — fixed me up with a little private tuition and took, I suspect, other measures to make me appear respectable from an Oxford point of view. Having been obliged to read the essays with which I had competed for prizes, he had formed, and expressed to me, the opinion that I might one day manage a *Coral Island*, but that a *Treasure Island* would lie beyond the twitch of my tether. The point of this very just remark was that both R. M. Ballantyne and Robert Louis Stevenson had been Academy boys.

Interim

I SEE THAT I have written as if, at the time of my quitting the Edinburgh Academy so oddly, and immediately thereafter, my going up to Oxford was a settled thing. But this — memory now tells me — was far from being so. Only two people, indeed, were quite clear about it: the Rector and myself. My parents, not always at one about their only child, both wanted me to go to Edinburgh University, and for the same reason: the plain matter of money. My mother, indeed, who had read Matthew Arnold's 'The Scholar Gipsy' among other things, felt an attraction to the Oxford idea, but it was she who told me —firmly if with a shade of sadness — that I would 'have to go' to Edinburgh. This was entirely sensible. I had declared for 'English', and in all Oxford at that time there were not, I think, more than a couple of scholarships held out to a schoolboy thus determined. So it would clearly be difficult for my father to find the sum required to support a commoner at an Oxford college through the three years of a degree course.

Faced with this situation, I showed myself, I have to confess, unscrupulous and ingenious. Early in that crucial spring, I put my parents in the family car and drove them round the cathedral cities of England. But I was careful to include Cambridge as well as Oxford. And, strangely enough, it was Cambridge that worked the trick with my father. We attended a lecture by a retired don, organized no doubt for the entertainment of tourists, descriptive of life at an English university. At dinner that evening, my father announced that he thought he could manage it.

And he did — although just how, I was never to learn. Perhaps a small tribe of indigent relations had to take a cut. About them, I wouldn't have cared a bit. But to my father, at least, I was to be eternally grateful.

There were formalities. The Rector had decided, upon inquiry, that Oriel would be the best college for me, since the 'English' tutor there, one Percy Simpson, was universally admitted to be a very deep scholar indeed. (What it was like to have a very deep scholar as a tutor, I shall come to quite soon.) So for Oriel I set off — and it was the first longish journey I had ever undertaken on my own — for the purpose of sitting the commoners' entrance examination. I had picked up a little about the place. I knew that I must say to the taxi-driver, 'Oriel, please', and not 'Oriel College'. (I may even have known that, had my destination been New College, it would have been proper to say, 'New College', and not 'New'.) But almost everything was, of course, unfamiliar to me. The examination itself was not exacting. I sat next to a Rugbeian, later to become an eminent Q. C., who was offering mathematics as one of his subjects. He glanced with evident distaste through the paper with which he was presented, picked it up between finger and thumb, and carried it off to the presiding don as something entirely disagreeable to him. What ensued was a flustered search through a pile of disordered papers in a hunt for something more to the candidate's liking. There was also a French unseen which began (I think), *Montez au Radcliffe Camera*, and was therefore likely to afford some slight difficulty to a candidate imagining a camera to be necessarily something one takes photographs with. (When one of my sons sat an examination at Oriel some thirty years later, the same French unseen was on offer.)

We were interviewed as well, and a young History don disconcerted and offended me by deriding an admiration I had declared for the plays of Bernard Shaw. But at this the Senior Tutor, who was presiding, took off his spectacles, nervously polished them, and diffidently but to an effect of overwhelming authority deprecated any endeavour to take the mickey out of nervous schoolboys. The Senior Tutor's name was David Ross, and he became my moral tutor when I went into residence. Rather later, he also became the great-grandfather of four of my grandchildren.

Between my leaving school and going up to Oxford a full year went by. During that year I had virtually no 'work' to do. From the University's simple entrance examination — then called, I think, Responsions — I was already exempt on the strength of certificates taken from the Academy, and I believed (not

31

altogether erroneously, as will have been seen) that any inquisition at Oriel would be a ritual rather than a test. I had nothing to do except buy books and read them.

I say 'buy' because of the peculiar character of the books already in our house. To my father the word 'book' meant a durably bound volume of *Scots Law Reports*, and when he exchanged legal practice for the administration of education in schools scores of these books arrived from his former office, to be ranged in a room which then ceased to be called the smoking-room and became known as the study. My mother's books included a good many that had belonged to her father, and one title-page is now in front of me. It is *Visions in Verse for the Entertainment and Instruction of Younger Minds*, and was published in 1751 as the work of Nathaniel Cotton, M. D. Cotton, I was later to discover, was the man who received into his private madhouse, and there treated kindly, the poet Cowper.

There were also a good many translations from approved ancient writers — Herodotus, Plutarch, Epictetus and persons of like kidney — which had been judged useful in the education of a young gentlewoman in the third quarter of the nineteenth century. I recall, too, *The Memorable Thoughts of Socrates*, and *The Golden Sayings of Marcus Aurelius*. There was also much Ruskin and Carlyle; distinctly avant-garde stuff compared with these.

None of this having been at all inviting — although it wouldn't have occurred to my mother that they could fail to engage my tender interest — I had had recourse, for my earliest reading, to such publications as a few pence would buy: *Magnet*, *Union Jack*, the *Sexton Blake Library*, and even *Comic Cuts*. My first glimpse that households existed more cultivated than my own had come from schoolfellows who intimated in class familiarity with Arthur Mee's *My Magazine* and a carefully polite comic called *Rainbow*.

I pause, and see that this exaggerates. Almost in my nursery I had been provided with the *Wonder Book of Ships*, and indeed with the Wonder Books of everything else. Governesses, moreover, had read this and that to me. But the general situation was distinctly not bookish. Then, on some occasion when I was convalescing from mumps or measles, my mother went out and bought me *Pickwick Papers* and *Rob Roy*. Scott wasn't an immediate success, but Dickens was a revelation. By the time Buckie Green was fulminating against me I may well have been, at least so far as novels went, the best-read boy at the Academy. My father, observing this proclivity, which he certainly didn't share, amazingly told me that he would pay any bookseller's bill that I presented to him. Every week I went into a bookshop on Princes Street to change my mother's 'library books' (we were bookish enough for that) and every week I there bought a book or books for myself. I bought them from a man called Harold; he had only one eye, but it was an eye for books and a boy who read them. Upon this, certain bibliophilic refinements followed. I discovered that the Oxford University Press had something called a depository or repository, also on Princes Street, and that if I took one volume of my leather-bound Thackeray there, a man would obligingly rummage and approximately match to it in hue the one I was about to buy. For some years I treated my books as physical treasures, ranging them and rearranging them on the shelves as if they were toy soldiers. Many people, by no means all of them scholars, preserve this attitude through life, treating a volume virtually as a chalice. Somewhere along the line, I have let slip this attitude to paper and print. Were I breakfasting with Wordsworth in Dove Cottage and he cut the pages of a book with the butter knife, my distress would be a good deal less extreme than was De Quincey's on such an occasion.

Oriel Bill

IN THE YEAR 1900, which was a quarter of a century before I went up to Oriel, there appeared a volume called *Memories of some Oxford Pets by their Friends*. I picked up a copy about a decade ago. The Sub-Rector of Lincoln, William Warde Fowler, like Lewis Dunbar a notable ornithologist, explains in a preface that these essays have been brought together by Mrs Wallace 'to win something for the sick and wounded in the war which has made the past winter such a sad one for us', and that her aim will be the easier to achieve in that 'Mr Blackwell has most kindly consented to undertake the work of publication without any profit to himself'. Warde Fowler urges upon hesitating browsers in Mr Blackwell's shop the consideration that 'animal life is assuredly worth study'. The university, I suppose, may be said to have acknowledged this fact 66 years later, when it appointed Nikolas Tinbergen as Professor in Animal Behaviour.

Some twenty Oxford people contribute to the book. The Right Hon. Professor and Mrs Max Müller report upon their dachshunds; a Mull terrier called Skian is the recipient of an important letter from Dr Birkbeck Hill, greatest of Johnson scholars; Tom of Corpus is celebrated in an English elegy by Sir Frederick Pollock and in a Latin elegy by Mr Plumer; a poodle called Puffles is commemorated in both verse and prose, and so effectively that in my own time as a senior member of the university his name had been transferred to a distinguished ornament of the higher clergy, a Suffragan Bishop of Dorchester.

One might expect *Some Oxford Pets* — a descendant of the keepsake books of the earlier nineteenth century — to contain a good deal of the sentimental and the facetious; in fact it exhibits humour, wit, vivacity, and an unforced lightness of air, and may be regarded as a small document of authentic significance in the history of Oxford taste at the close of Victoria's reign. It pleases me that pride of place in it is given to Oriel Bill. The only illustration, a frontispiece, is a handsome photograph of Bill provided by Mr Soame, who was still in my undergraduate time photographing (gratuitously but speculatively) those of my contemporaries who were achieving precocious fame at the Union Society or on the river, or even within the Examination Schools of the university.

Bill was a bulldog, the property (or friend) of A. Wootten-Wootten of Headington and Oriel, with whom he lodged for a time at 15 Oriel Street. When Mr Wootten-Wootten attained to the B.A. degree and departed into the world Bill lingered on amid the scenes and faces he had come to love. In his later years, like other retired Oxford worthies in Headington and similar purlieus of the town, he became a little chary of too frequently dropping in on his old college. For long, indeed, he turned up only for the greater festivals: a habit which unfortunately resulted in a growing addiction to the pleasures of the table. But he continued to know every member of the college, and would go with an Oriel man anywhere, while to all others turning a deaf ear. Having earned a just celebrity not only with the learned and investigating classes but with the citizenry at large, he was at all times able to hail a hansom cab when he required to be driven home. He earned high distinction on the stage when undertaking the part of Launce's dog in an O.U.D.S. production of *The Two Gentlemen of Verona*. But eventually we learn that, 'on May 22, 1898, he suddenly dropt down in a fit; all that loving hands could do was done, but he was past help, and now he sleeps in a corner of the college that he loved so well.' And already an elegy had been composed for him. It is not a very good elegy, but it contains, at least, one memorable line:

Thou need'st not go to Schools, immortal dog!

Provost

THE MEMOIR OF Oriel Bill was contributed to Mrs Wallace's
volume by the Revd L. R. Phelps, who in 1914 was to become
Provost of the college. He was one of the first acquaintances I
made when I arrived as an undergraduate commoner. He was a
hospitable man, who faithfully discharged his duty of entertaining the junior members of his society in bunches and on a
systematic basis. Being a good conversationalist in a somewhat
allusive mode, however, he took particular pleasure in tête-à-tête
occasions with juvenile interlocutors possessed of sufficient
miscellaneous reading to know what he was talking about. I must
have filled this bill quite well, since I can't recall ever having been
in his presence in the company of another undergraduate. And
since I was very shy, the Provost may moreover have judged me
(fallaciously in fact) incapable of much convivial association with
my contemporaries, and have been the more inclined to take me
up as a consequence.

Dr Phelps was a venerably bearded man, very liable to inspire
even more than an appropriate awe. When I went to tea with him
in the Lodging it was occasionally to find him entertaining some
scholar more venerable still. At one early tea-party it was the
great Dr Paget Toynbee, then regarded in Oxford (whether
accurately or not, I don't know) as the first of living authorities
on Dante; and Dr Toynbee received a tremendous dressing down
for having turned up on a brief visit to the university without
having included evening clothes in his stock of attire. The tea
ceremony was itself intimidating, rather in the fashion that a later
generation associated with the receiving of that civil refection
from the hands of Miss Ivy Compton-Burnett. The equipage
included china which had perhaps belonged to the Provost's
grandmother. Certainly he cherished it very much. He began by
letting fall into each saucer, with a maximum of precision, a
single drop of hot water from a heavy silver jug held in an aged
but well-poised hand. I supposed this hydrostatic performance to

be in aid of fractionally increasing friction or adhesion between saucer and cup, thereby minimizing the risk of humiliating misadventure on the part of a guest doing a balancing act on his knees.

But the Provost, although adept at giving an appearance of leisure to social occasions, was not by nature of a sedentary habit, and he had developed numerous resources for speeding the departure of those young men (always a majority, whatever their background) who were unable to get to their feet and take their leave. Thus at tea-time he would lead the conversation towards some athletic topic, from this to the college games field, and from this again to the subject of badgers — which he would aver, quite baselessly, to have established a set endangering the cricket pitch. He would then recall Sir Thomas Browne's holding in debate whether or not badgers have longer legs on one side than the other, this the more readily to scamper round hills. Next, he would suddenly recall that a portrait of a badger hung some-where in the Lodging, from which the truth of this matter might conceivably be verified. The picture would be located after a walk through the ramifying house; the badger would be seen to be equipped as other quadrupeds are; and then one would discover that the picture hung beside the Provost's front door, which stood open before one. The proper words would be spoken, and one was out in the irregular public space which the college was later going to persuade the municipality to give a name to as Oriel Square.

Dr Phelps's after-dinner technique was simpler. He would wait until, from the adjacent Tom Tower, Christ Church began to bang out the hundred-and-one peals with which — with some justification immemorially antique — it assaults the city nightly at five minutes past nine o'clock. The Provost would thereupon stand up and shamelessly declare: 'Ah, my dear boys! The witching hour of twelve has struck.'

I have said that the Provost was no sedentary man. He was in fact a formidable pedestrian, and he marched me over as much of the countryside round Oxford as I have ever traversed since. On Sundays, however, his favourite walk was merely up the hill to Headington, where at that time there was situated what I imagine was still called the Workhouse. He had sat on the Poor Law Commission of 1905–1909, and in vagrancy in particular he maintained a keen interest. So we would set off of an afternoon for a chat with the tramps. The walk through Oxford could be slightly embarrassing, since the Provost was given to greeting totally strange passers-by as a squire might greet his cottagers. To men he would raise his blackthorn stick and call out 'Good day to you, my master!' and to women he would touch the brim of his large black straw hat. On these Sunday expeditions I felt I ought to wear a hat myself, and as there was no time to doff it to every female thus encountered I was reduced to the brim-touching technique too, and self-consciously felt it to be extremely ludicrous. The tramps, however, were enormous fun, since Dr Phelps possessed the art of drawing them into a free if not very articulate conversation. There was one, from Yorkshire, who claimed to remember the Brontës — and who, it was evident, did authentically remember legends about them. 'Ah — the lad!' he said. 'He was the wild 'un.'

Dr Phelps was himself good at remembering, and on the walk back to college might entertain me with reminiscences of Matthew Arnold and John Henry Newman. There was frequently a satirical slant to these, particularly when he was dealing with Arnold. One story, much detail of which I forget, was of Arnold's driving out to Blenheim to call on the Duke of Marlborough, entangling his boot inextricably with some patent unfolding step of the conveyance, and writhing helplessly before a line of frozen flunkeys, with the duke himself looking on, equally immobile, at the top of an enormous flight of steps. It was not, I think, the Provost himself who told me how, as a very junior fellow of the college, he was despatched with a group of more senior Anglican clergy having the delicate task of congratulating a former fellow on becoming a prince of the Holy Roman Catholic and Apostolic Church. Young Phelps broke the ice by advancing upon the new Cardinal of St George in Velabro with outstretched hand and the words, 'Well done, Newman, well done!' I believe anecdotes like this a little startled me, Arnold and Newman standing in my mind as the chief glories, by no means thus to be frivolously dealt with, of the by now not particularly distinguished college in which I found myself.

Phelps and his successor in the Provostship, my moral tutor W. D. Ross, a much more intellectual man, are the only dons I can remember taking much account of. Ross told me at some brief beginning-of-term interview, when I had no doubt been talking pretentiously about my reading and opinions, that it seemed to him that a great deal of nonsense was written about literature. Because he said this at once diffidently and with authority (as I had reason to recall his being able to do), I received it as a maxim at once, and have applied it with great benefit in my dealings with critical expatiation ever since.

Preparing for the First Public Examination

In 1925 the majority of undergraduates who, like myself, were not aiming at the sort of final grandeur of such things as the Honour School of Literae Humaniores, spent their first two terms in preparing (rather than being prepared to any substantial extent) for a kind of rag-bag examination in diverse subjects in which there was a considerable element of choice, and which nobody took very seriously. I might have chosen English Literature as one of these, but was advised (presumably by Ross, my Moral Tutor) not to waste my time on this trifling approach to the severities of what was to be my Final Honour School. So I got up — so far as I can remember — the *Poetics* of Aristotle in a translation; the *Agricola* and *Germania*, together with a selection of the letters of the younger Pliny; some French, including Corneille's *Polyeucte* and de Tocqueville's *L'Ancien Régime et la Révolution*; and Political Economy, for which there was a single textbook, beyond which we were not encouraged to stray.

On all these there were lectures going in one corner of Oxford or another. Being a tolerably conscientious boy, I attended a good many of them, scurrying round on a bicycle from one to another. They were a mixed lot. A man with the notable name of Marcus Niebuhr Todd, an Oriel don and the college's other Moral Tutor, did his best with young Pliny. Todd was charming and endlessly enthusiastic, and diverted us by instantly breaking off his discourse if a young woman arrived late in his lecture-room, and confounding the poor girl by making a concerned to-do over finding her a comfortable seat. But Pliny remained quite awful; somewhere or other he had a villa; and he expatiated on the beastly place to an effect of intolerable boredom for pages on end. To this day — although my house, as it happens, is probably on the site of a Romano-British homestead running to one or two mosaic floors — the news that the remains of a complete Roman villa have been discovered within a comfortable walking distance would prompt me to no more than burying my nose in a book. It

was different with Tacitus. Half a dozen lectures brought him
alive for me. *De origine et situ Germanorum* sounds unpromising
enough. But *tam diu Germania vincitur*! Even Buckie Green's old
pupil kindled to that.

To my pot-pourri of subjects there was added the Examination
in Holy Scripture. Whether it was technically part of the First
Public Examination, I don't know. But nobody could proceed to
any sort of B.A. degree at Oxford without having passed either it
or — by special dispensation — an equivalent examination in
some other major and generally recognized religious faith. This
examination — commonly called 'Divvers' — one could sit for
pretty well when one pleased, and among undergraduates there
was held to be a definite impropriety in passing it at a first
attempt. Almost, here was a solecism as grave as wearing a
'made-up' bow tie. I was very aware of this, and a conformist
instinct in me made me determined not to succeed at my own
initial appearance. So I wrote a paper, or papers, in consonance,
as I felt, with the general idea. There was, however, a *viva voce*
examination, in which I had to sit down before three or four
gravely attentive clergymen who put questions to me — entirely
without gaining a satisfactory response. But then the senior
examiner produced a trump card. 'Mr Stewart,' he asked
suddenly, 'can you tell me the Apostle Peter's other name?'
Taken by surprise, I said, 'Simon, sir', and became aware of nods
of approving assent from all the clergymen on the job. I had, after
all, passed Divvers.

During those first two terms — if I remember aright —
Oxford's celebrated tutorial system impinged upon me only in
one of the subjects in which I was to be examined: Political
Economy, nowadays known as Economics. There happened to
be in Oriel at that time a young don so new and so conscientious
as to believe that an hour ought to be devoted to me *solus* every
week. So every week I wrote what must have been virtually a
childish essay on some aspect of Political Economy for this don,
Eric Hargreaves, and read it to him in his rooms in Oriel's
Rhodes Building. Hargreaves listened with complete attention,
and then contrived to discuss it with me precisely as if we were
two professional economists chatting together over nuts and
wine. Raw though I was, I don't think I failed to mark the
virtuoso character of this performance. There was only one
diversion — which, however, occurred fairly regularly. The

Rhodes Building fronts Oxford's High Street, and every now and then it would shake or shudder in a manner faintly suggesting a premonitory hint of coming earthquake. All that was actually happening was the passing down the High Street of some particularly heavy van or lorry. But it caused Hargreaves' door to rattle. And when this happened he would raise a hand to suspend our deliberations, turn to the door, and firmly call out, 'Come in!'

Another misconception for some time attended these occasions — connected, however, not with Hargreaves' door but with his staircase. Regularly pounding up this with the near-lateness which I had gathered to be the prescriptive way of attending tutorials, I frequently brushed past an elderly man whom I might well have knocked down had he not stepped back and made way for me with what I took to be a respectful bow entirely becoming in a college servant, and whom I therefore rewarded with a breezy 'Good morning!' as I swept past. It was some time before I was apprised of the fact that this well-conducted (and surprisingly agile) senior was not, in fact, the staircase's scout but the Regius Professor of Modern History, H. W. Davis. He was, as it happened, as much a new boy at Oriel in 1925 as I was, Oxford having a peculiar system whereby a newly appointed professor may have to transfer himself to a professorial fellowship in a hitherto alien college. Davis had been, among other things, editor of the *Dictionary of National Biography* — which was one day to describe his 'manner' as 'reserved but modest'. I'd have said it was exactly that.

Tutor

A SCHOOL OF English Language and literature had existed at Oxford since 1894, but was of little account until the appointment of Walter Raleigh (a former Academy boy) as a professor ten years later. Raleigh faced a situation in which a rapidly increasing number of undergraduates was seeking for regular tuition largely in vain. Governing bodies throughout the university doubted the subject's constituting an adequate academic discipline; judged it likely to promote no more than 'chatter about Harriet' (a phrase attributed to the historian E. A. Freeman) and were reluctant to expend money on the establishing of tutorial fellowships to deal with the situation. Thus challenged, Raleigh took vigorous steps, and one of them brought me my own tutor, Percy Simpson.

Simpson was at the time a middle-aged master at a school few had ever heard of, but he was also a fully-equipped classical scholar who had begun to make a name for himself in the application of an exact textual criticism to English literature of the Elizabethan period. Raleigh discovered that the Clarendon Press (which is the learned branch of the Oxford University Press) was hard up for a proof-reader who could cope authoritatively with Greek and Latin, and he judged that Simpson, if brought to Oxford, might fill the bill while at the same time helping with the tuition of such undergraduates reading English as one or another college might send to him.

Walter Raleigh was a *littérateur*, and it is much to his credit that he thus introduced a severe scholar to the Oxford English scene. But for Simpson the going was tough. He was married, with two children; totally (but here I have to guess) without private means; and already dedicated to the editing of the works of Ben Jonson with a rigour that Shakespeare alone had hitherto received. And now as a tutor, if the guineas were to come in, he had to work very long hours indeed. He was, of course, when I came to know him, a fellow of Oriel (but a 'supernumerary' fellow, whatever that may have meant). Yet if there was to be jam as well as butter at home, he had to devote what used to be called weekly 'private hours' to anything up to 30 young men who came, one at a time, to read essays to him.

That he *did* listen, I haven't the slightest doubt, although I am a little short of memories with which to back up this conviction. I recall, from many years later, an Oxford colleague assuring me that it isn't necessary to listen to a man's essay. Indeed, he asserted, sometimes, and with the best will in the world, it isn't *possible*, since there are voices so somnolent in suggestion that one is certain to fall asleep while listening to them, be their burden what it may. But — my colleague continued — there need be no occasion for panic: the silence when the essay-reading is over is bound to wake one up, and one can then lean forward and say, in a slightly menacing tone, 'Would you mind reading that last sentence again, please?' Abashed and slightly disconcerted, the young man obeys, and from this sentence the quality and indeed outline of the whole essay may be diagnosed with a sufficiency quite adequate for reasonably useful discussion. The tutor, in fact, is rather in the position of the French anatomist Cuvier, who from a fragment of bone could infer with certainty the bizarre structure of an entire prehistoric monster.

Percy (as his pupils all called Dr Simpson among themselves) never asked for such a repeat performance. What succeeded upon the reading of one's essay was invariably a long, and totally unnerving, silence. When, at my first tutorial, I experienced this, I supposed, not unnaturally, that my new tutor was asking himself what point in my miserably insufficient effort it would be most useful to comment on, whether kindly or otherwise. But what did come from Percy, with an inexpressible husky *gravitas* and air of cogency, was a question. 'Did I ever tell you,' he asked me, 'what Meredith said to Sidney Colvin?' I said, 'No, sir' — promptly but in some bewilderment, since I was conscious that there had been no previous occasion upon which this information could have been accorded me. 'Meredith and Colvin were in conversation,' Percy went on weightily. 'And Meredith said to Colvin, "Colvin, they tell me there are passages in which my poetry may be charged with obscurity." And Colvin' — and here Percy solemnly chuckled, so that I felt instantly obliged to contrive a solemn chuckle too. 'And Colvin, delighted at the sudden opportunity, took from the shelf a volume of Meredith's verse, opened it upon a certain passage, and handed the book to the poet. And Meredith simply laughed.' At this point I became aware that Percy's whole person had been overtaken by what can only be termed a silent laughter of his own, and I was trying to emulate this difficult concatenation when I saw that Percy had instantaneously become entirely solemn again. 'And then,' Percy said, 'Meredith said to Colvin, "Concentration and suggestion, my dear Colvin! Concentration and suggestion are what I aim at in my poetry."'

Most of my subsequent tutorials with Percy Simpson bore more or less the same character as this initial one, and it surprises me, looking back, that there is nothing bleak and fruitless in my memory of them. Their *ambiance* was certainly bleak enough. Eric Hargreaves had been a young man living in college, and he had taught me in a room which (although it shuddered)) was reasonably appointed as a living-room. Percy's working room in college was very small, and entirely square; it contained a small, square table; two hard and upright chairs on adjacent sides of it; an ash-tray (for Percy smoked frequent and — as it seemed to me — unnaturally small cigarettes); and a small, empty bookcase. I am perfectly certain that there was nothing else *whatever*. Very occasionally, if he was stumped for a date (but his head was full of dates) Percy would turn to this bookcase, appear perplexed in a weighty way, and murmur that it had for long been his intention to have 'a concise reference library' on its shelves. His erudition seemed to me enormous. But there was an explanation: the English syllabus at that time stopped short at, I think, Matthew Arnold, who died in 1888, and round about that date Percy's interest in English literature stopped short too. Thus, although many of his pupils, including myself, knew 'The Waste Land' more or less by heart, I am almost certain that he had never looked into it. Moreover, he simply nominated at the close of one's private hour the following week's work. 'Your next essay,' he would say huskily as one took leave of him, 'will be on Shelley.' And that was that. When I myself became a college tutor I used unwarily to ask my pupils to choose the succeeding week's writer. Whereupon some well-read boy might say 'Clough', and I'd realize that, doubtless culpably, I'd never read even 'The Bothie of Toper-na-Fuosich'.

Incidentally, the story of Meredith's profound utterance I must have hastened to circulate among my fellow undergraduates, since I own a volume of Donne's poetry and selected prose which must have come to me as what we called a 'twenty-firster', on the fly-leaf of which the donor, Nigel Abercrombie, has written, 'Concentration and suggestion, my dear Colvin'.

Excursions on Memory

PERCY SIMPSON, BEING presumably, like John Bunyan, of 'a lowly and inconsiderable generation', didn't have in his store of anecdotes any based on precocious encounters with notabilities long since dead and gone. It was, of course, from the Provost, Dr Phelps, that I received these. Much later, I was to receive many more, Oxford being rather fond of such linkages with the past. A number of them turned on a President of Magdalen called Martin Routh, who had died in 1854 in his hundredth year. It was obvious that Routh must have remembered people who could remember events in a very remote past indeed: Charles II, for example, walking down Oxford's High Street attended by a leash of spaniels. Less startlingly, my colleague at Christ Church, Sir Roy Harrod, the economist, recalled being patted on the head by Henry James in the courtyard of Burlington House. There was nothing very out of the way in that, and I could cap it with the information that one of my aunts, when living in Chelsea, had been accustomed to travel in the same omnibus as Thomas Carlyle. More strikingly — for I am now writing in 1986 — I once met a man of whom it was claimed that he had fought against Napoleon in Egypt. I thought of him as an Arab, but have no doubt that he was called a Mameluke — in the sense in which the word is used to mean something like 'conscript' or 'fighting slave'. The future Emperor at the Battle of the Pyramids was confronted by 60,000 of these, and it is probable that a small number of the survivors lived to be very old men. But this survivor, if genuinely what he purported to be, must have been very old indeed. That he abundantly looked the part, my memory emphatically asserts. I shook hands with him, and his hand was ice-cold and bony, so that it frightened me. I think my father had to pay an extra shilling to gain me this experience. It cost a shilling to file past and a further shilling for the hand-shake, since the ancient creature, all but mummified, was a side-show in some sort of circus. About the circus itself, which must have been far more agreeable, I recall nothing. Yet I am certain of the ground upon which it was pitched. It comes regularly on television screens whenever an international Rugger match is played at Edinburgh. Instead of the ephemeral big top of the circus there is now an enormous concrete stadium open to the sky. Perhaps a goalpost plunges into earth at the very spot on which my Arab still lingered tenuously within his tenement of clay.

I have done some sums, beginning from the fact that Napoleon left Egypt for Paris in October 1799 and the conjecture that a boy could, in a sense, have fought against him at the age of fifteen. The *Dictionary of National Biography*, consulted on the celebrated 'Old' Parr, is found to carry a cross-reference to Henry Jenkins, who undoubtedly died in 1670, and claimed to have been born round about 1501. He claimed, too, to have been, like my Arab, something of a soldier, at least to the extent of having carried a load of arrows to Flodden Field. If the claims of these latter-day Methuselahs were reliable (which, unfortunately, they are not) there would be nothing of extraordinary note about my encounter with the Arab.

But I have a more sober story. In Adelaide, South Australia, I used to take tea with a lady who had been familiarly acquainted with the man who helped John Keats to the little Latin he knew. Keats died in 1821. The man was Charles Cowden-Clarke — the son of the poet's schoolmaster — who lived to be ninety. The lady was a Miss Howard-Clarke, who as a young woman (not a child) had domesticated for some years with her kinsman Cowden-Clarke in his old age in Genoa. It was Cowden-Clarke's wife, Mary Cowden-Clarke, who achieved the first complete concordance to Shakespeare. I have a copy of the second edition of her book in which a previous owner has inscribed the date 1875.

And here another large spanning of time may be recorded. On Friday, February 14, 1986 I attended in Westminster Abbey a service in memory of Philip Larkin. This was a little more than 58 years after I had witnessed, again in the Abbey, the burial of the ashes of Thomas Hardy. Only a few months before his death Larkin had mentioned to me in a letter his 'wonder' that Hardy's funeral was within my memory. Larkin had been born in 1922.

Much of the detail of that earlier occasion I have forgotten. How, for example, did I come to be in the Abbey on Monday, 16 January 1928? It must have been within a week of the start of my

Margaret Stewart

Margaret with Michael

In Leeds, with Michael and Nigel, 1935

John and Margaret Stewart

Fawler Copse

final Hilary Term at Oriel, and somebody must have obtained a ticket for me, since I was able to walk straight in through a considerable crowd outside, and be shown to a pew with a clear view of what Hardy himself would probably have called 'the enactment in question'. The crowd is mentioned by the second Mrs Hardy in an appendix to Hardy's oddly disguised autobiography. She also says that it was cold and wet, and I remember that too. She records the presence of 'representatives of the King and other members of the Royal Family'. I don't remember them.

But I do remember the Gods of Modern Grub Street. *Gods of Modern Grub Street* was the singularly tasteless title of a book I had greatly cherished not many years before the occasion I am now recording. That it is no longer on my shelves may be due to its having been good-humouredly mocked by Norman Cameron, one of my more sophisticated Oxford friends about whom I shall presently have something to say.

Here, suddenly, they were! Barrie, Galsworthy, A. E. Housman, Kipling, Shaw — to say nothing of Percy Simpson's pet aversion, Edmund Gosse: these men advanced majestically escorting Hardy's remains up the aisle, with Stanley Baldwin and Ramsay MacDonald leading them, and a couple of dons from Oxford and Cambridge respectively bringing up the rear. Shaw struck me as peculiarly translucent, perhaps as a consequence of his vegetarian habit; he reminded me of one of those very-deep-water fish which carry their own little electric generator around with them. Galsworthy seemed not quite at ease; perhaps he felt that, as an English gentleman, he ought to know his way around an Anglican church, but had rather forgotten the drill. Kipling, disconcertingly, appeared to be the spit image of a caricature of Kipling by Max Beerbohm.

Thomas Hardy's *remains*. One had to remind oneself that what Mrs Hardy calls a 'compromise' had been effected. Hardy's heart had been removed for burial among other Hardys in the churchyard at Stinsford in Dorset; in Westminster Abbey the impressive catafalque provided for that escorting file of eminent persons concealed only some urn-like object adequate for the rest of Hardy after cremation at Woking. A good many years later, Wystan Auden told me that there had, in fact, been no burial at Stinsford. They had been a little careless about the heart, and the Max Gate cat had got away with it. This story justifies itself in the retelling only because Hardy himself would have liked it. It is very much his sort of thing.

The curiosity of these two Anglican occasions turns on the fact that neither Thomas Hardy nor Philip Larkin was a professing Christian. Nor can they quite be called 'agnostics'. They did believe they *knew*. Hardy could at times wish 'it might be so', but he was quite clear that it was not. With any bright believing band he had no claim to be, since he saw in himself:

> but a thing of flesh and bone
> Speeding on to its cleft in the clay.

Larkin was similarly absolute, only at times harsher. Religion was 'created to pretend we never die'. Yet both men were 'churchy' in a very real sense of the term which the *O.E.D.* will be found failing to capture. Hardy was given to suggesting to callers a walk over to Stinsford 'to view the various graves'. Larkin in 'Church Going' records that he often visits churches; is 'much at a loss' to explain the habit; and superbly catches the bafflement in his most famous place:

> Hatless, I take off
> My cycle-clips in awkward reverence . . .

For a memorial service more has to be devised than for the burial of the dead. Once the ashes of Thomas Hardy had been brought into Westminster Abbey the Book of Common Prayer took over, and the known persuasions of the dead man were irrelevant to the occasion. It wasn't so with Philip Larkin. He had taken pleasure in jazz, and so a jazz band twice briefly performed for us. He had written about jazz, so something from that writing was read aloud. But very much more significant, of course, was his rejection of all that theology teaches. And here the Dean and Chapter — if the expression be not too crude — took the bull by the horns. We were at once bidden to give thanks for Larkin's 'intellectual integrity which would not allow him to accept the consolations of a faith which he could not share and which would have delivered him from a fear of dying by which all his life he was haunted'. And that fear, we were told, was finally 'dispelled', since Larkin 'now shares our rejoicing in eternal life'.

After this the Poet Laureate read the Lesson and Jill Balcon three of Larkin's poems, and the final prayer was by another English poet (a Dean of St Paul's), John Donne.

Like Webster in T. S. Eliot's poem, Philip Larkin was much possessed by death, and a kind of grim frivolity was sometimes his note, as it is often Hardy's. In the letter I have mentioned, he describes the service in memory of John Betjeman (for whom he had a deep affection) as 'an extraordinary occasion . . . like a vast cocktail party only without cocktails'. This extravagance would not have occurred to Hardy, who nevertheless might have been prompted (at least as a poet and not as the frequenter of smart gatherings) to an almost similar sardonic stance. But Larkin has recorded that it was another Hardy who was sovereign with him: the Hardy of 'Thoughts of Phena at News of Her Death'.

If Roy Harrod was patted on the head by Henry James, so might I have been (if appropriately positioned) by George Meredith. I thus belong as near as makes no matter to the Late Victorian Age, and therefore recollections that do not strike me as exactly from the dawn of life seem occasionally to strike my friends as much more remarkable than I myself find them. For example, I have a clear visual memory of the Grand Fleet at anchor above the Forth Bridge in the early years of the Kaiser's War. And that I understood what it guarded us from seems to me attested by the fact that, returning from Australia at the end of 1945, I burst into tears at my first sight of a White Ensign flying east of Suez. But I am no antiquarian. Coins and shards and broken columns please me in a fashion but don't especially move me. I have already mentioned that here where I live beneath the Berkshire downs there was a homestead in Romano-British times. Philologists tell me that the very name of my house attests the fact; my Saxon predecessors murmured it wonderingly to one another as they peered at the mosaic pavement from which a spade may still turn up the tesserae. But I am far less remote from the prosperous farmer who treated himself to this metropolitan prestige-object than he was from the earlier people whose broken pots and flaked flints it amuses my acquaintances to pick up from under our feet as we walk. All this is good for conversation, and, when modestly obtruded upon visitors, elicits gratifying attention. But my imagination responds more readily to our snails, which are larger than one commonly meets with in England. The Romans are reputed to have introduced them as an appetizing *hors d'oeuvre*. Here they are still, and here they have always lived: generation upon generation of sentient creatures that have never known the instinct to emigrate; never been exterminated in war or by predators or through disease. It is unenterprising in me never to have organized a Lucullan banquet making a start with them in the French fashion.

Yet this awesome continuity of organic life fails, on scrutiny, to amount to much. My snails, being hermaphrodite, copulate reciprocally, and may be said to own parents, although not a mother and father. Yet it is unlikely that they carry through life any memory of these immediate progenitors, although generations of remoter ancestors must be owned to have built into them intricate patterns of instinctual behaviour. They are certainly unfortified or unburdened with thoughts of a future in any significant sense. The staggering discovery of that lies further down evolution's road; it comes, as Meredith says, to intelligences at a leap, on whom pale lies the shadow of the tomb.

Unlike the snails — or even, one supposes, the clever dolphins — we know that within a hundred years (or say a hundred and fifty, to allow for my Mameluke and similar Old Parrs) we shall all be dead. *All of us.* Mnemosyne has had her brief hour upon the stage; her last speech delivered, she withdraws into the wings. The play, indeed, preserves a kind of *liaison des scènes*, and 'living memory', like Mr Poole's myriorama, gains from one roller as it loses on the other. But always the view is equally confined, and of what disappears as Time turns the handle there is left only gut knowledge, oral tradition, painted caves and kitchen middens, written records and (nowadays) electronic storage and retrieval systems. Without these, civilization as we think of it would collapse. Yet how unstable, how unreliable is the whole vast fabric of recorded knowledge! The history books are full of mistakes and contradictions and lies. Scientists are perpetually changing their minds. It is far from certain that Jesus of Nazareth was at all like the man depicted by Holman Hunt, or his mother like the woman known to Raphael or Piero della Francesca.

The snails are presumably content with what they have themselves run into, or are at the moment running into. We want more. We have developed a certain hunger (insatiable and hydroptic in a few) for knowledge for its own sake. In a narrower regard we want at least some element of predictability about our future, and we search our experience for what it can here — all uncertainly — provide. But — oddly, situated within the tide of time as we are — we may feel it to be our past that is most important to us. Steadily through that past we have been built up from our mewling and puking stage, and in that past we search for our identity.

The severe form of amnesia known as hysterical fugue is said to be a rare condition, but one comes upon it every now and then at least in an anecdotal way. Tennyson's father, going to pay a call on a parishioner, is said to have forgotten his own name as he stood on the doorstep and rang the bell. He had to take a turn through Somersby and be greeted by a rustic before it came back to him. We all forget people's names in an unaccountable manner, but nearly always recover them when we have ceased to try, and Dr Tennyson may be regarded as having turned this mechanism briefly inward upon himself. But the same morbid condition may last for a considerable time: a man will vanish for weeks and be in entire ignorance about himself until restored to familiar surroundings, and in some way reconciled to the self he has been seeking escape from. Such vagaries of the mind readily offer themselves as the material of fiction. Rebecca West's first novel, *The Return of the Soldier*, is about an officer from whose memory the stress of battle has obliterated many years of married life, so that he believes he has come home to resume an idyllic love affair with another woman which in fact had ended long before. It sounds a tall story. But at Slateford War Hospital, not far from where Rebecca West had been at school, W. H. R. Rivers and his colleagues were at that time coping with effects of 'shell-shock' quite as bizarre as this.

The essential ego of our life is a product of memory. The narrower and more uncertain our recollections, the less secure is our persuasion that somewhere within our carcasses (which are in a perpetual process of flux) and harbouring amid our thoughts (which are as fluid as water) an 'I' securely exists. Without this sense of an 'I' we cannot at all make do. There are psychologists who declare it to be an illusion, or at best a species of spaghetti-junction. All the same, if we lose faith in it we go dotty.

There is much nowadays that prompts us to worry about memory. Its fallibility, known to every judge who has to listen to conflicts of evidence over events of common life, can be alarmingly demonstrated in laboratories. Simple misquotations, such as earned us reproof at school when we had not got up our 'repetition' properly, turn out to reveal sinister processes at work in the recesses of our minds. For years I believed that Marlowe's Jew of Malta went abroad of nights and kicked sick people groaning under walls. In fact he killed them. And kicking is more simply sadistic than killing. So what a nasty man I am.

The depth psychologies go one better, having evolved the concept of the screen memory. I distinctly remember my first discovery of the facts of female anatomy as occurring when a small girl-cousin came running downstairs from her bath with her dressing-gown flying, pursued by a scandalized nanny. But I have invented this, or at the most borrowed it from some entirely insignificant occasion, to stand in place of something much more dreadful that happened in a wood-shed. And indeed I am perpetually inventing a past self. It isn't, curiously enough, in the least in the interest of creating a paragon. Richardson's Sir Charles Grandison, who had the knack, if we are to believe his creator, of moving uniformly well through a variety of trying situations, in fact probably peered into a past abounding in deeds of the most murky order. They may all have begun as phantasies, but later he undoubtedly ceased to be aware of this, and he ended up believing many of them to have been veridical.

We search memory as our forefathers searched conscience, and from a similar motive. Does the record sum us up as sheep or as goat? Are we justified and saved, or are we reprobate and damned? Only in our time we have secularized and (I suppose) trivialized the question, since what we seek to see as saved is not soul but self-esteem. Is it an impressive person that I glimpse as I peer down the vista of the years, or is it a Prufrock? Hamlet, or an attendant lord? With a sinking heart I realize that this is Prufrock's own sort of question. Or say that I leave my colleagues at a late hour. They are serious men. They don't write books in the hope of affording somebody a few hours of harmless amusement. They are much more intellectual than I am. But for the moment I am not oppressively conscious of this. I have been quick and gay and resourceful in chitchat, and only to the correct level have I been flown in wine. A delightful evening and — let me be frank with myself — I was a success! I wind down the window of my car to wave on another vehicle; a surprisingly chill wind blows through; *suddenly I see myself.* For here is a sometimes fiendish characteristic of retrospection: present in the recaptured scene is one's very self, precisely as if an independent spectator were now viewing it. And how factitious is that vivacity; how over-insistent that securing of attention; how aweful this or that momentary failure even to remain decently well-bred! Prufrock, indeed! Almost at times the fool.

Wystan Auden told me, near the end of his life, that he could recall absolutely nothing disagreeable that had ever happened to him. And although he had much trafficked with Freud in his time he rejected the notion that there was anything insalubrious in this suppressing of painful experience beneath the level of consciousness. It was, he believed, one of Nature's better ideas, and he was convinced that it is widely operative among men. I am inclined to think the contention holds a certain limited truth. But most of us, I imagine, remember the major disagreeables, at least those in our adult experience, well enough.

Oxford and Oriel Again

THE OXFORD UNDERGRADUATES of the 1920s belonged as much to a pre-revolutionary era as they did to a post-war one. It had been widely believed that such a cataclysm as the Kaiser's War would be bound to bring radical changes to the university. In some colleges the dons held a nervous fear that a returned young soldiery, of whom there were expected to be many, must prove unruly and even licentious. They recruited, under various academic disguises, officers from the Brigade of Guards as experts in disciplinary action. But in fact little that was disruptive occurred. For one thing, the demobbed warriors proved to be less numerous than had been expected, for the sufficient reason that they were dead. Those that did come proved more orderly and industrious than the boys straight from school. There was a general disposition simply to get things going again. Within a few years nearly everything was re-established and as it had been. The Oriel I entered a few days after my nineteenth birthday in 1925 — when, of course, most of those returned soldiers had gone away again, — can have differed in no marked particular from the Oriel of twenty years before. The social composition of the place was the same: preponderantly public school, and taking the manners and assumptions — not always admirable — of gentlemen's sons for granted. It was also taken for granted that, although there were plenty of menservants around to empty our slops and carry meals and coal-scuttles up to our rooms, we were essentially schoolboys still, and to be governed accordingly. We were segregated from the other sex on a curiously taken-for-granted basis which was a somewhat unrealistic hang-over from how it had been at school. 'Womanizing' of a low sort was regarded by most of us as unspeakable. There was popularly believed to be one solitary prostitute operating in the city, but nobody had ever seen her. She was known as 'Delight' and must have been named from within the English School, since it was John Keats who had asked:

What more felicity can fall to creature
Than to enjoy delight with liberty?

Romantic heterosexual attachments and even cautious experiments — but all preferably disastrous — in distant places and
during vacations were admitted and occasioned mild awe; but
one risked ridicule by a bare mention of the women's colleges
already flourishing in the university.

There were further antique conventions. We were locked up at
night. We had to attain a fixed quota of attendances in the college
chapel under penalty of being punished in various annoying and
trivial ways, the chief of which was being 'gated'. This meant
being locked up of an evening earlier than the rest of us.

There was a further odd segregation when we dined in hall, the
clever men having to sit at one table and the other men at others.
In the main, I suppose, this last ordinance (which may, here and
there, still exist) led to people the more readily finding themselves in congenial society. But it enhanced the notion of scholars
and commoners being races apart, and its application in individual cases could be absurd. I can recall Ronald Syme, a mature
student from New Zealand who was later to become Camden
Professor of Ancient History and a holder of the Order of Merit,
having thus to associate nightly in a sort of dunces' gallery almost
exclusively with callow youths whose conversational range was
confined to matters of athletic or social concern. In this instance,
indeed, I remember the result as pleasingly comical, the future Sir
Ronald being unable to conceive of any human being as other
than passionately interested in classical antiquity — and talking
uninterruptedly, with aggressive brilliance and disarming
charm, in the confidence of this fond persuasion.

My own acquaintance were varied in point alike of ability and
temperament, but rather fell down in terms of any broad social
spectrum. Oriel didn't at all go in for aristocrats, nor for the sons
of very wealthy people, and it did harbour the sons of a few very
poor ones. This latter fact, admirable in its way, I suppose to have
been of the Provost's contriving. One of his unlikelier stories was
of the college's Governing Body once having contemplated
pursuing Thomas Hardy for libel on the ground that a vignette
on the title-page of *Jude the Obscure* seemed to represent our front
quadrangle, and might thus suggest that it had been by one of his

own praepostorial predecessors that Jude Fawley had been insolently repulsed. Dr Phelps, a man of family at least to the extent that one of his grandfathers had been a fifth baronet, had been at school at Charterhouse, and saw to it that there were always a good number of Carthusians among the public schoolboys who, as I have mentioned, formed the bulk of the college's undergraduate members. But his interest in what used to be called the 'social question' (and rather more a deep charity hidden away in him) was always active. There was one contemporary of mine who, having written to him artlessly and from an obscure situation to inquire whether residence at Oxford could be managed on (I think) £30 a year, found himself railroaded into the college at once. He attained in later life to a prominent position as a dramatic critic.

Of course Oxford, like every ancient university, began as an informal association of poor scholars, and for centuries there was almost nobody else around. Later, when the colleges turned substantially into preserves of the prosperous, the penniless lingered on as servitors and sizars or the like, and finally as boys living on small scholarships and charitable grants. I can't say that in my own time this made any sort of edifying spectacle. Considerable gifts of the spirit and intellect are required to counter severe economic disadvantage within a community; and in Oriel, as long before in Samuel Johnson's Pembroke, there were a few young men whose poverty cut them off from too much that was going on. A marked amelioration in this state of affairs has been one of the major gains of the later twentieth century. Plenty of students are hard up, but below a certain minimum of subsistence nobody is depressed. If you are rather poor you at least have plenty of company.

In 1925 it can't have much helped those without money that money went a long way. The majority of us, living on modest allowances like my own, pursued a course of life which would now be regarded as within the reach only of the opulent. We treated each other to quite elaborate luncheon parties in our rooms; dined at the George restaurant, where there was the excitement of watching the current celebrities, headed by Harold Acton, come and go with immeasurable exhibitionistic flair, or drove out to the Spread Eagle at Thame, where Mr John Fothergill afforded us a grand sense of *grande cuisine*, with bills to match. I recall at the Spread Eagle a glimpse of Evelyn Waugh, only lately gone down from Hertford, and already the author of one of the funniest novels in English. He was slim and fair and far from over-dieted. We certainly didn't yet think of him as immoderately sequacious of acceptance within the upper reaches of society.

But I fear we had our own snobberies. We spent quite a lot of time (it seems incredible today) in expensive clothes, and our shoes came from a superior shop in the Turl. We smoked cigarettes rolled in black paper, or tipped with gold, or in some similar way distinguished from the fags of the common herd. The pictures on our walls had often been done one at a time by artists favourably noticed in sixpenny weeklies.

For most of us, of course, there was an honest shoe-string element in the hinterland of all this fleeting magnificence. I myself used to get by on the strength of purchasing Francis Meynell's latest Nonesuch Press books from Harold in Edinburgh at the end of a vacation, and selling them eight weeks later for a larger sum to Mr Sanders in Oxford High Street. The profit paid for a railway ticket home, and there I'd sit down and do a good deal of work — certainly enough to keep my chin above water as what an earlier generation called a reading man. All this was very normal and unremarkable.

I sometimes wonder why I don't look back on that phase of life with more affection than I do. One reason must reside in the simple fact that the undergraduate's is inherently a melancholy condition: a state of affairs doubtless constant from generation to generation, and connected with the general ignominy of growing up. One can get awfully glum. Norman Cameron, a Fettesian and a very good poet, whom I had known on a neighbourly basis at home, and who for a time had rooms across the staircase from mine in Oriel's front quad, had a habit of breaking in on me in the small hours, making enough noise to wake me up. He would then simply stand and gaze at me in unfathomable dejection. This stasis was at least reassuring, and I had little difficulty in matching his mood at once. After some five minutes of such mute communion Norman would shamble away again, closing the door very softly, as if I were still asleep. His depression may have been enhanced because his scholarship was in some way connected with a Bible clerkship, which meant that he had to appear regularly in the college chapel for the purpose of reading the lessons. His perception of the world's sadness at times a little seduced him from wholly temperate courses, and there was an occasion upon which he advanced to the lectern and pronounced the words, 'Here beginneth the Gospel according to St George.' The Provost from his stall helpfully ejaculated, 'John, boy, John!' But Norman, almost as if he were a scholar in the most senior sense, was reluctant to admit error in a matter of fact. 'Here beginneth the Gospel according to St George,' he reiterated firmly. 'In the beginning was the word . . .' And he read on in the rumbling sleepy voice which I can still hear when I read his verse.

At home, and living within a few hundred yards of one another, Norman and I were, for some time, much in and out of each other's houses during vacations. (It was almost as it had been with my schoolfellow Jim only a few years earlier.) But eventually it was borne in on me that I was disapproved of by Norman's widowed mother. I was puzzled by this — and reasonably so, since I was at least a well-mannered youth. The reason, when it became apparent, was an odd one, and related to an article of dress of which I was rather proud. This was what we called an 'up-to-the-necker': a light jersey with a high roll-down top which obviated the need to wear a tie. My up-to-the-necker was silken in appearance and of a delicate shade of mauve, and I think it may have had slender silver threads interlaced with it here and there. So, conceivably, Norman's mother had a point — although a totally mistaken one — when she decided that here was the very sort of young man who might assail her son's virtue. That Norman at that time had a virginity to lose (except, indeed, in some such aberrant manner as Mrs Cameron was envisaging) I had — as will presently be seen — conclusive evidence to disbelieve. Indeed, only a little later, he somewhat eccentrically provided himself with a mistress, whom he freely introduced to all his acquaintance.

As a consequence of Mrs Cameron's curious misconception, Norman and I, for a time, met most frequently in my own house. I had by now appropriated the 'study' exclusively to my own use, and in his good-humoured way, it amused Norman very much. In Edinburgh I was still a much less sophisticated boy than I cared to reveal myself in Oxford, so here my walls were smothered with Art. There were two enormous photographs of the west fronts of Amiens and Rouen cathedrals respectively; an equally large sepia reproduction of *La Belle Ferronnière*; several full-size Medici colour-prints; and rank upon rank of smaller approved masterpieces which I had myself framed with the aid of a stuff called passe-partout. There may also have been several little plaster copies of the Venus of Milo and similar charmers. Norman dubbed the resulting ensemble my 'prig room', and was fond of carrying me off from it to the Caledonian Hotel at what Edinburgh calls its West End, where we would sit in the lounge drinking whisky and soda. For himself, Norman told me, this regimen had been medically prescribed. And then one day he got to his feet and announced, with his curious suggestion of a deep and not quite concealed enjoyment of life even at its most tiresome, that he had better go and have one of his 'painful pisses'. Oddly enough, I understood this at once, and was mildly horrified but deeply impressed.

My next, and last, full memory of Norman Cameron — by which I mean a memory with clear visual pictures attached to it — must date from nearly ten years later. Like Wystan Auden, Norman had gone to Nazi Germany and there married a young woman who thus became a British citizen whom he could bring back with him. She was a nice girl, and Norman was behaving nicely to her. But that he had any particular interest in her didn't, in what was rather a brief encounter, at all appear. Norman obtained employment with an advertising firm, and died in 1953.

High Tables

THIS BRIEF ACCOUNT of university days and ways affords an appropriate point at which to bring out of the drawer something that has lain there for some time. Perhaps four years ago, I received a telephone call from New York. Would I write a short piece on Oxford's High Tables? The call came from the office of one of the great newspapers of the world, and I accepted at once. The commission was far from requiring anything to which could be given the dignified term of research, but I did rummage here and there in more or less familiar places. The piece went off, and almost at once there came another telephone call. It was explained to me (very definitely for the first time) that my effort had to take its place in a series devoted to *cuisines* — so would I alter my offering accordingly? Happening to hold (I think with the late Lord Stockton) that good food is to be appreciated but not talked about, I excused myself from this difficult proposal.

But here, already in this preamble, is an intolerable deal of sack to one half-pennyworth of bread. So to my little essay:

'Sir, it is a great thing to dine with the Canons of Christ-Church,' Johnson told Boswell during a visit to Oxford in 1776. It must certainly have been formidable, for Cardinal Newman (who inquired into the subject) records that, there in the 1770's, the Canons sat down at their high table at 3 and remained there till chapel at 9. At other high tables similar habits obtained. At Oriel, where Newman was one day to be a fellow, the Provost 'was continually obliged to be assisted to bed by his butler', and an unfortunate undergraduate Bible clerk had to say grace upon the conclusion of this performance before being allowed to dine himself. Edward Gibbon, unlike this lowly youth, entered Magdalen as a gentleman commoner, and was in consequence admitted as an equal to the society of the fellows. 'I fondly expected,' he writes, 'that some questions of literature would be the amusing and instructive topics of their discourse.' He was disappointed. 'Their conversation stagnated in a round of college business, Tory politics, personal anecdotes, and private scandal; their dull and deep potations excused the brisk intemperance of youth.' But the seniors could be rowdy at times as well as dull. Gaudies or college feasts, Newman told the young Mark Pattison, were 'a scene of wild licence'.

Dinner at high table was a formal, even if at times a bibulous, affair. One had to turn up punctually and exhibit correct table manners. Again at Oriel, James Tyler as Dean 'sent away four men for coming to high table too late', and Edward Coppleston as Provost reproved Newman for refraining from wine and rebuked him for proposing to 'help sweetbread with a spoon'.

Two hundred years after the visit of Johnson and Boswell, dinner at high table still marked for some Oxford dons the beginning of the serious business of the day. It is described in college statutes as the 'common meal', and you have to dress properly for it. I once heard anxious debate on what is implied by this. Some speakers were for a post-war resuscitation of dinner-jackets; others for abolishing them except upon the most august occasions. Or suppose one got into evening clothes only on Saturdays and Sundays? This would be an innovation, a stout minority maintained, undesirable as being unrelated to the normal behaviour of English gentlemen.

When, in the middle of the nineteenth century, fellows of Oxford colleges were allowed to marry, they scarcely altered their habit of celibate evening refection. One gets the impression that in the later Victorian period many admirably domesticated men hardly ever missed their dinner in hall. This gruesome sundering of husband and wife, father and child, at that violet hour when ordinary families come together, has been fading out in recent years, and luncheon has in effect been taking over from dinner as the common meal. It seems a trivial change, but a learned paper would be required to relate it adequately to the larger spectacle of social revolution in England.

What about all that brilliant talk at high table which novelists of university life are so fond of? Does it really happen, or are the dons still Gibbon's dons? Here are, say, from a dozen to thirty men (only now it is likely to be both men and women), all of them presumably intelligent, and with a wide spread of intellectual and scientific accomplishment between them. Much of their conversation is bound to be interesting, and some of it is likely to be amusing. But does it abound in what we commonly think of as wit? I don't think it does — and for a reason very characteristic of the Oxford scene. By Oxford's standards you don't become a wit by practising yourself at clever talk; what you become that way is a bore. Wit is an innate endowment, and its deliverances have to start up in the mind like a creation. It is no prerogative of the highly educated, and we do well to do without it rather than accept a mere colourable substitute. In Oxford, everybody is agreed, there are never more than some half a dozen wits flourishing at any one time.

Some years ago senior members of the university gathered for the funeral of a Warden of All Souls, whose name was Sumner. They waited, and the coffin appeared. Whereupon the Warden of Wadham turned to his neighbour and murmured, 'Sumner is icumen in'. Perhaps it is frivolous to admire such a freakish joke. But its wit, if minuscule, is spontaneous and sheer, and Oxford delights in that.

'Schools'

THE OVERWHELMING MAJORITY of young people who went up to Oxford in the 1920s did so in order to learn more about a subject that had interested them at school, and to get a degree. Some, of course, seduced by this or that, or perhaps compulsively attracted to political or literary or artistic interests which the academic scheme of things failed to allow for, fell by the way. Others, although they got degrees, didn't get 'good' degrees; and a substantial minority eventually got either 'poor' degrees, or no degrees at all. And all this I imagine to be substantially unchanged 60 years on.

Occasionally we learnt with awe of some spectacular rebellion. At Cambridge, we heard, a young man called Christopher Isherwood had been sent down for presenting his examiners with nothing but extemporary sonnets, and indecent sonnets at that. Our own Norman Cameron claimed to have been presented with a paper to which, on his conscience, he had been unable to respond other than with the words, 'Horace was a bad and superficial poet' — no more and no less. (It is possible that in recounting this Norman exaggerated a little, for the examination was one which he certainly survived.) But I have a rather different memory of another poet.

In my own final Schools I happened to sit almost facing Wystan Auden, and so had a glimpse of him in tears. This was astonishing, even unnerving, but there could be no doubt about it: the tears were coursing down his pale and ample, if as yet unfurrowed, cheeks. The explanation lay in his feeling that he was letting his tutor down. There were special circumstances here. Wystan had gone up to Christ Church proposing to read Medicine, drifted indecisively from School to School as terms ticked by, and had finally been rescued, late in the day, by Nevill Coghill, an 'English' (but also Irish) tutor of whom he had become very fond. So behind the sense that he had let Nevill down was the sense that Nevill might feel that he, Nevill, had let

Wystan down. When Wystan told me, so many years later, that he could recall nothing disagreeable as ever having happened to him, I wondered if he had indeed lost all memory of those tears in Oxford's Examination Schools. He did, of course, get some sort of degree. Had he failed to do so, he would have been unqualified to become the university's Professor of Poetry in 1957.

It must have been one day in July 1928 that I emerged from the Schools with my *viva* in this same examination behind me. It had probably lasted for some ten or fifteen minutes — enough time for all four or five examiners to show themselves more or less benevolently disposed, although only one of them, J. R. R. Tolkien, regarded me with any very obvious interest. Out on the pavement of the High, I was fairly sure that I had got a First from them. But somehow I wasn't particularly elated. I may even have been realizing that, thus all abruptly, I was among the number of the unemployed.

Not knowing what I was going to 'do' was a state of mind already familiar to me. My mother had cherished for a time the notion that I might become a minister of the Kirk, like her brother-in-law, James Stewart. I doubt whether I had ever regarded this as other than an absurdity, but it did bring me a couple of years on a crash-course in Greek at the Academy — which I have always regarded as the best thing in an educational way that the place did for me. The Rector was aware of my problem, and on the same occasion upon which he had ventured the conjecture that I might manage a *Coral Island* he had gravely spoken the following words: 'You know, Stewart, what happens to boys who don't know what they want to do in life. They become chartered accountants.' About *Coral Island* he was more or less right, and his subsequent remark, although unflattering to what I understand to be an arduous training and useful pursuit, may have reflected a hovering thought that, like himself, I belonged with the race of scholars, after all. (Dr Ferard had been a fellow of Keble as a young man.)

But — unemployed! There wasn't a doubt of it. Of course, even at Oriel, a small college, there were men 'going down' at that time about whose future there was already no doubt at all. There was Ronald Syme. There was James Meade, a top-flight economist. To men like them fellowships and chairs already beckoned. But there was also A. J. P. Taylor, a year senior to myself, and reading History. It happened that he was my closest friend, but I don't think it is because of this that I saw him as being as able as anybody on the horizon. It was, however, a profoundly discontented sort of ability. He believed that at Oxford he had 'learnt precisely nothing'. Its History School increased one's knowledge of history while entirely neglecting an understanding of it. Oxford had simply been an obstacle to getting on; and, in order to get on, Alan had first eaten dinners for a couple of years at the Inner Temple and then — after gaining his First — had become an articled clerk in a flourishing solicitor's firm owned by an uncle. There would have been a good deal of money in this in the long run. But from the first day he realized that he had made 'a ghastly mistake', and after six months he broke his articles and escaped. So Alan was unemployed, just as I was.

Alan then discovered that he was a historian after all — but not, I think, that he was to be as brilliant as any in his generation: inwardly he was as diffident and misdoubting as outwardly he was tough and arrogant. Getting into the relevant Establishment and back to Oxford wasn't easy for him, particularly as he had no impulse to lower any flag he might have a fancy for sailing under. This being so, we decided it would be perfectly reasonable to top off a university education with a kind of Grand Tour, and we set off for Germany and Austria accordingly, accompanied by several other members of the unemployed class. The foreign exchange was so odd at that time that we were virtually unconscious of financial impediment. In Vienna — always with some like-minded youths coming and going — we spent upwards of a year; and only when we returned did gaps open up between us. A certain Charles Gott ceased being a scientist and became a gentleman farmer; Geoffrey Rowntree (our Cocoa King) learnt to become a schoolmaster; Peter Mann just disappeared — presumably into the City. I brought back from Vienna some ability to skate, and a decent (Austrian cavalry style) seat on a horse. Alan, somewhat contrastingly, had mastered Austrian diplomatic history from Metternich onwards.

I began to feel decidedly lonesome as an unemployed person.

WORKING LIFE

Chance

AND THEN A chance befell: a casual and fortuitous thing. It was decidedly that. Alan Taylor claimed — on what grounds I don't know — some acquaintance with Francis and Viola Meynell, who a few years earlier had started, along with David Garnett, the Nonesuch Press. So I found myself at a party given by these typographically and bibliophilically distinguished persons. The Meynells and their friends were distinctly a Bloomsbury crowd, and I found the party bewildering and quite outside my experience. Meynell, seeing the misdoubting youth isolated in a corner, came up and made conversation. He was the most courteous, as well as the kindest, of men. Among his current projects, it appeared, was an edition of one or another translation of Montaigne's Essays. Gathering that I had read English at Oxford, he politely consulted me about this. It so happened that I possessed the relevant patter, and I rattled off the dates (1603, 1613, 1632) of the three editions of John Florio's pioneer translation, adding my considered opinion that it was much superior to Charles Cotton's later effort of 1685–86. Instantly, Meynell invited me to edit Florio for him.

This, in itself, was quite sensible. I had a little kept my head above the dark waters of academic oblivion by winning a prize for which young Oxford graduates could compete, and I possessed a genuine confidence in myself on that sort of belletristic ground. Unfortunately, I added on the spot my conviction that the Nonesuch Florio ought to be a 'critical' edition — having in my head, no doubt, something like Percy Simpson's Ben Jonson, which must then have been about half-way through the 40 years or so it took to achieve. Meynell at once agreed — seeing, I think, technical interest in the handling of a long march of variant readings.

I hurried off to Oxford. Percy Simpson was delighted. He regarded the Nonesuch Press as sharing a kind of Satanic region with the blameless if displeasing Edmund Gosse (a pretender to learning) and a disreputable unfrocked priest called Summers. (Had not Summers unscrupulously preyed upon the Asiatic innocence of Mr J. C. Ghosh in that murky business of an edition of the plays of Thomas Otway?) So Percy viewed me as a young Heracles about to cleanse the Stables of Augeas in darkest Bloomsbury. After something over a twelvemonth he still commanded my name, but had forgotten, I think, that I had been a mere undergraduate pupil of his, and not one of those (to my mind, rather dull) post-graduates who had pursued under him what he liked to call the 'Advanced Studies', and were thereby equipped to deal with Elizabethan texts in an adequately scholarly manner. So Percy in his turn hurried off — in his case to the key men on the Governing Body of the College. His recommendations always carried weight because they were invariably nothing if not temperate: 'his essays were prepared with care' was the best I ever got from him in an end-of-term report to the Provost — which was a bit dim as well as being, to my own knowledge, not particularly true. So now I found myself abruptly elected into some sort of Senior Scholarship at Oriel, to which an emolument was attached for a couple of years. And as Francis Meynell was a liberal paymaster, I became, while settling down in shocking ignorance with John Florio, better off than I was going to be for a very long time thereafter.

But where was I going to do the work? Had I known the ropes better, I could, I believe, have returned into residence at Oriel and got on with the thing in the Bodleian Library. I had, however, now been living in London for what I regarded as a long time — probably as much as six or seven weeks — so I elected for the Library of the British Museum. And there, because one of the volumes of Florio I wanted to collate bore on a fly-leaf the inscription 'Willm̃ Shakspere' (judged by some well-reputed scholars to be an authentic signature), I was at once promoted to work, not in the enormous circular reading-room sacred to the memory, among others, of Karl Marx, but in an awesome inner sanctuary known as the North Library. When actually engaged on this particular book I was required to sit under the immediate regard of an elderly and vastly responsible library clerk. Everybody in the North Library except myself (or, to be accurate, and as will appear, every male person) was decidedly elderly. I judged the mean age to be about seventy, but this may have been an exaggeration.

So here I arrived every morning shortly after nine o'clock, and toiled on until bells rang and the place closed down at some evening hour. I lunched in a little Greek restaurant in a side-street close to the Museum, and where I dined I don't know. With a scholar's proper modesty, I had found myself an attic room in a lodging-house somewhere in the region of Belsize Park. It was a stiff climb up, but I didn't mind that. What did come to worry me a good deal was the long drop down. If I began to walk in my sleep, and walked through the window, John Florio would remain undealt with, so far as I was concerned.

That I was thus going a little mad came seriously to worry me, and I took the wholly reasonable step of seeking an early transfer to the ground floor. And there, presently, one of the two or three bed-sits became available. It was going to be a good deal more expensive — surprisingly so, considering it was no larger than the room I sought to quit. But presently I learnt the reason. Ground-floor rooms were much in demand by gentlemen who liked to have a lady friend drop in on them unobtrusively once or twice a week. I did make the move, and was very soon all too closely acquainted with this social phenomenon. In *Der Zauberberg*, Thomas Mann has his hero, Hans Castorp, run into almost the identical situation early in the novel. Hans Castorp's reaction to the pantings, spankings, gaspings and giggling audible through the wall of his room in his cousin's sanatorium is entirely one of distaste and disdain; good-naturedly, he tries to put a harmless construction on them, and when this fails he decides that honour forbids his taking any cognizance of such unseemliness. I can't at all believe in this, since in Belsize Park the whole thing compelled and excited me very much. Suddenly, and in a manner hitherto unfamiliar to me, sex was rearing its ugly head. So I was a step yet nearer to going dotty. Friends from Oxford and elsewhere took to turning up on me at week-ends in a helpful way. It had become evident that I required taking out of myself.

This state of affairs was ended quite suddenly by Peggy. Peggy lived in Eltham, a region unfamiliar to me, but worked in the North Library: she was that sole exception to the place's being frequented only by aged, or at least elderly, men. What Peggy did there, I was never to discover, since she was reticent about it. It must have been some sort of quite humble large-scale copying, since Peggy wasn't at all well-educated. I spoke to her. I took her out to tea, and explained myself. Soon I was taking her to films and to the theatre. Rapidly, I changed my manner of living, leaving Belsize Park to become briefly a sort of paying guest in the flat of a motherly woman, the well-left widow of a trade union boss, now established in a big block of apartments with a very splendid name: Westminster Palace Gardens. I was still very lonely there. I had a portable gramophone from my schooldays, together with a few records: I spent hours listening again and again to the *Eroica* Symphony. My widow, deciding I was anaemic, plied me with a stuff called, I think, Bemax. Tiring of being thus mothered, I moved across the court to a small service flat of my own. (Meals were brought to me on demand two or three times a day: it is astonishing that, there at the end of the 1920s, on what was a small budget still, that sort of thing was entirely within my means.)

So there to my heart's content I could entertain Peggy to tea, detaining her until the very last seemly train from Charing Cross to Eltham. And all this was entirely innocent. Even when we went boating on the Serpentine and were caught in a downpour, so that Peggy had to get out of her own clothes (which I can recall crassly calling her 'finery') and into some of mine while hers dried out before the electric fire, it remained that, or virtually that. And, meanwhile, Florio went swimmingly.

It was only after some months that I gathered that in Eltham Peggy had an appropriate swain who was turning a little restive. This was disturbing intelligence, and I did begin to wonder whether I was treating my girl friend altogether well. This, however, coincided with other news in a convenient fashion. The Nonesuch assignment was near its end; I had the duty of looking for a more permanent job; and the job came along. So there was a parting of the ways. Yet a vague discomfort remained with me. I was quite sure that Peggy had never heard of Prufrock. I wasn't so sure that she hadn't been in contact with a sibling of his.

Chance Again

I HAD PUT in for a couple of posts as a junior lecturer in civic universities, and had in each case received a punctilious letter from a professor explaining why, for one reason or another, the job was going elsewhere. But at a third attempt I achieved an interview. It was at the university of Leeds. So to Leeds I went, and on the morning after my arrival found myself in a room with three other young men. Two of them were Oxford graduates, and the third was a graduate from Cambridge. We made conversation while, no doubt, trying to size one another up. A clerk came in with a big black bag from which he proceeded to disburse our expenses. Mine was the largest claim, because I had put up in Leeds's most expensive hotel. No unfavourable notice was taken of this, although for an alarmed moment I thought it might be. We were then interviewed in — I suppose — alphabetical order. Certainly I was the last of us to present myself to the appointing committee. It consisted of the Vice-Chancellor, who was a grim Scot called Sir James Black Baillie, and the professors of English Language and English Literature respectively. The Vice-Chancellor took a strong dislike to me almost at once. I don't think I resented this, since I had a wholesome notion of myself as pretty intolerable in various ways. And actually, the small fact of this man Baillie's displeasure was to bring me the principal blessing of my life. Of this, of course, I hadn't a clue. But I did have an instant suspicion that if the two professors were agreed about a candidate then the Vice-Chancellor would have to give way. So to F. P. Wilson and E. V. Gordon I did my best to produce sensible answers to any questions they put to me. After rather a long interview I was asked to return to the waiting-room. So there were the four of us together again. I seem to remember that now we had nothing further to say to one another. I could hear my watch ticking. Then the man who had carried the black bag opened the door, and asked Mr Stewart to return to the committee room. Thus, even before I had sat down again opposite Sir James Black Baillie, I knew I'd got the job. Sir James, who was clearly displeased, confirmed the appointment briefly, and told me — or as good as told me — that he himself had had enough of me, and that I could take myself off. It was then that the apocalyptic thing — as it was to turn out — happened.

Professor Gordon, who was a quiet Canadian of unassuming manners, seemed to feel that this wasn't quite on, and that some civility should be offered me. So he got up and followed me to the door, where he murmured to me that I might presently be hunting for digs, and that if this were so, he had a recommendation to make. He himself, before his recent marriage, had digged with a Miss Rowe, as indeed some other members of the university staff had done. It might be a good idea if I had a look at what she could perhaps offer in the way of accommodation. And he gave me the address. So there and then I took a taxi — for I had unsuitably large ideas about that sort of thing — and sought out Miss Rowe. And yes, Miss Rowe had a sitting-room and bedroom available, and was very happy that the privilege of occupying them should go to somebody recommended by Professor Gordon. She already had three guests. Two of them were brothers, the sons of some Yorkshire grandee. The third was a medical student. She married me some twenty months later.

So if it hadn't occurred to E. V. Gordon . . . Most people, I imagine, have had occasion to make this kind of reflection. Generalize from it, and you arrive at a distinctly daunting view of the slender extent to which any man controls his own destiny, and of the unpredictable effect of any such destiny upon a ramifying future. I now have twelve grandchildren. Without E. V. Gordon I might still conceivably have twelve grandchildren, but they would be a different lot. So not only would my own circumstances have been radically changed; an increasing number of people's destinies would be affected right on to the end of time. The tremendous Greek term εἰρωνεία covers this, and is at its most potent when 'dramatic' — when the ignorances surrounding us produce a situation with an issue opposite to that which we expect from it. There is here a large scope for gloom. Thomas Hardy was particularly fond of exhibiting in this section what he called life's little ironies.

★

It wasn't, of course, thoughts like these that I carried away from my interview. I went back to the Queen's Hotel and up to my room. I packed my suitcase, and then I looked out of the window. It was above the level of most of the adjacent roofs, so there was an extensive view of shabby and smoky Leeds. I felt I had never seen so beautiful a city. As well as being a city, it was a future. I suppose that was the way of it.

There was a knock on the door, and F. P. Wilson entered. He was a diffident man, but without ado he picked up the suitcase. I must spend a second night in Leeds; we could talk about the coming term's work — but in his own house, where his wife was expecting me. So, still with the professor as porter, I went down in the lift and paid my bill. We got on a bus — not into a taxi — and arrived at the Wilsons' home. Before dinner, I had to go up to the bedroom of their two sons and be introduced, since the small boys were demanding to see the man daddy had 'choosed'. On the following morning the work of the English Department was, I suppose, explained to me, although of this I have no memory. I went back to London in the afternoon, and arranged to terminate my tenancy in Westminster Palace Gardens.

Leeds

THE UNIVERSITY OF Leeds was two years older than I was, but existed previously as the Yorkshire College, which had provided instruction in the arts and sciences applicable to the manufactures, engineering, mining and agriculture of the county. It still looked like that when I arrived. There had, indeed, been one fairly recent innovation: the erecting, against a wall close to the principal entrance, and presumably as a war memorial, of a large work by Eric Gill, executed in his favourite *mezzo rilievo*, representing Christ's casting of the money-changers out of the temple. Sir James Black Baillie — very sensibly, to my mind — had lately ordered the growing of a screen of ivy over this inappropriately sited artistic object. There was a central building, purpose-built in 1885, together with many terrace-houses in adjacent roads, which had been taken over and devoted to one department or another. In one of these, known as English House, I shared an attic room with a senior lecturer called Wilfred Rowland Childe. Nearby, two villas had been run together and were called Staff House. Here there were several common-rooms and a refectory. It was all very unpretentious, and entirely agreeable. The university of Leeds today is much more imposing. Particularly striking is the new library. But to this particular accession there attaches a certain note of comedy, to which I shall come.

The other centre of my new life was Willow Cottage, the property of Miss Rowe. It lay in the suburb of Headingley, was much older than most of what surrounded it, and rather too large to be called a cottage with any propriety. Miss Rowe was a gentlewoman and locally well-connected: notably, if a shade mysteriously, with the Tetleys, a family brewing most of the beer drunk in Yorkshire, and distinguished in various other ways. Miss Rowe's connection with the university was old-established, particularly with former members of my own department. Ronald Tolkien is, I suppose, the only one of them to have entered the halls of fame, but to a fledgling like myself the roll was impressive. For the proper entertainment of her lodgers Miss Rowe relied utterly on the only servant in her establishment, a woman in middle life whom she invariably addressed as Luffman, but who was known to all the rest of us as Luffy. Luffy was superb. She worked from dawn to dusk without a pause, and every evening put on a splendid dinner. I don't remember that anybody helped her with the subsequent washing-up; and Miss Rowe would certainly have vetoed anything of the sort instantly. Luffy was devoted to everybody who came her way; everyone liked her; but everyone took her labours for granted.

I had a further stroke of luck in my first weeks at Leeds: that of forming an almost instant friendship with Denis Binyon. Denis was, like myself, an assistant lecturer: in Latin, although he liked Greek rather better. He had been brought up in circumstances totally different from my own. His father had curated something in the B.M., and his home had been somewhere in the *aedes annexae* of that august institution. He had gone to school at Westminster (where he had been ingeniously tortured by other boys in a gym) and then up to Merton. Yorkshire completely bewildered him. In whatever direction he looked, perplexity assailed him. There was, for example, an economist of some seniority amongst us, and this economist referred to his children as the 'kiddies'. Was such a thing believable? Denis had once been pursued round and round a table (this had nothing to do with Yorkshire) by a promising musician with what was plainly amorous intent. What on earth was one to make of that? There was always a touch of apology about Denis's confessing to these incomprehensibilities. But he was convinced that a person so vastly well-traded in the ways of the world as myself would understand them at once. So what did I think?

I had no power to do any thinking for Denis on the larger mysteries of the human situation. But I did discover that Miss Rowe had yet another bedroom going, and I got him installed in it. We shared the sitting-room, and also a great many flagons of South African red wine. We might well have been taxed with regressive behaviour. Recent undergraduates routinely ejected from Oxford, we tended to see ourselves as Ovids among the Scythians. (Denis had rather more excuse for this than I had, since at least his uncle was a distinguished poet.) We were critical of many of our senior colleagues as encountered in Staff House. I had found the following in a volume of verse by some virtually unknown poet dating from the later eighteenth century:

> His mien was awkward; graces he had none;
> Provincial were his notions and his tone.

To whom in the university of Leeds might this be most fitly applied? Denis opted for the man who called his children the kiddies. But marriage and children of our own lay straight ahead of both of us.

So much for Denis Binyon, and his chronic mild perturbations. Wilfred Childe, contrastingly, was the most comfortable man I have ever known. In his twenties he had been of some note as a poet of the avant-garde, but had exchanged this (in search, no doubt, of comfort on a spiritual plane) for conversion to the Roman Catholic Church, celebrating the fact by becoming Wilfred Rowland *Mary* Childe, and shifting to verse of a more traditional sort. He and I attended Denis's wedding together, the sacrament transacting itself in a Wesleyan chapel. Entirely inoffensively, Wilfred treated the occasion rather as if it were a visit to a zoo, and being unable to call the place a 'church' settled for its being an 'ecclesiastical edifice' — this with an amused consciousness of whimsical intolerance. Wilfred had an enormous capacity for immobility and idleness; he could sit for hours in the enjoyment of these luxuries; yet he was never intellectually or aesthetically dozy, and he showed at need a quick and correct sense of the ludicrous. He has a niche (I am afraid) in an early Michael Innes novel called *The Weight of the Evidence*; and the university of Nesfield as there portrayed owes something to the university of Leeds. But Leeds was some twelve thousand miles away when I wrote the story, and viewed from that distance had taken to itself outlines of a drastically farcical sort.

Thumbnail sketches are all very well in their way, but a clutch of them begins to show as a kind of irreverence to the dead. So I must try to shift from personalities to occasions in this account of my academic days in Yorkshire. My own first occasion was perhaps the giving of a first lecture. I had, of course, never before given a lecture. I had never made a speech in a debate, except once — and with a singular lack of success — at the Academy. At Oriel I hadn't so much as read a paper to a literary society, although I had engaged in a great deal of play-reading. So here was a quite new thing to be done. My professor, F. P. Wilson, had clearly addressed his mind to the question. I was to do no lecturing in my first term, during which getting the hang of how to conduct tutorials would be quite enough on my plate. But then, I think, Wilson had a further thought. A first lecture is a worrying thing, and the more worrying the longer one has to think about it. So it might be best to spring a sudden emergency upon me — and this he contrived. In a week's time, he murmured to me, he had unfortunately to be absent from Leeds for a day. So would I much mind going in to a certain large class and giving a lecture — just a single lecture — on Byron? And any approach I chose to take would, of course, admirably do.

The psychology of this was, it is quite clear to me, impeccable. A job had to be done, and there was no time in which to get fussed about it. So I sat down, and wrote out a lecture in full and with proper care — which was to be my habit, indeed, for more than 40 years. I didn't lack material. I had read a lot of Byron, and also a lot *about* Byron, biographically considered. I even had a theory, which I fallaciously believed to be my own, about one of the main puzzles here. His bride, apparently far from discontented with her lot, had gone happily home to her parents on a short visit following upon the birth of her daughter, and immediately among the Milbankes all hell had broken out, with lawyers and alienists called into consultation. It seemed obvious to me that Annabella (although, indeed, prim and interested in mathematics) had artlessly confided to her mother what she took to be no more than amusing eccentricities of sexual behaviour on the poet's part. I wasn't unaware that a certain delicacy was required in touching upon this, and I took considerable care over the framing of the few sentences required. On reaching the lecture-room, however, what immediately confronted me was a row of half a dozen nuns on the front bench. Unaware that ladies who have entered religion are about the last people in the world to be discomposed by the vagaries of sex, I felt that a perfectly awful situation confronted me. Could I cut the offending passage without revealing the fact that something had gone wrong? Was the entire lecture tainted, tasteless, insalubrious? I wasn't happy for a moment during the whole performance. When I ended, one of the nuns, aware that here had been a young man on his feet for the first time, came forward and expressed her own thanks and that of her companions for the instruction and pleasure they had received from me. At Oxford we had been accustomed to refer to nuns, monks, and the clerical classes generally as religious caterpillars — a phrase coming to us, I think, from Christopher Marlowe by way of T. S. Eliot. I have nearly always found them to be singularly courteous people.

Those were days before television and the ability, at the flick of a switch, to summon distinguished and talkative persons into one's home. So public lectures by wandering celebrities were of regular occurrence and usually well attended. I recall three in particular. The first lecturer was Humbert Wolfe, a civil servant from Whitehall who wore his hair long, presumably to show that he was also a poet in his abundant spare time. His verse was, in fact, very popular, and he had considerable power of destructive epigram — announcing, for instance, of Galsworthy, that:

> . . . like his books, the soul of John
> Goes on, and on, and on — and on.

What I most clearly remember of Wolfe's lecture is its peroration. Jerking back his abundant locks, and raising both arms high in air, he cried, 'The angel of poetry is abroad in the land! I can almost hear the beating of her wings.' There was, undoubtedly, a slight confusion here. For an earlier poet, John Donne, angels are sexless (*Difference of sex we no more knew/Than our guardian angels do*); for Milton, although apparently susceptible to amorous inclinations, they are uniformly male; not even the most resolute feminist has thought of making wenches of them. Muses, of course, are female: all nine indubitably are. But not even Melpomene, perhaps the most soaring, is credited with wings. Some of us, no doubt, scoffed at this absurd trope of rhetoric on Humbert Wolfe's part. My thought was for F. P. Wilson, who had at once to get to his feet, and produce a few scholarly remarks in moving a vote of thanks.

My next lecturer (and there is an ascending order of consequence here) is I. A. Richards. We all felt him to be formidable — intellectually formidable quite beyond a common scholar's capacity. In *Principles of Literary Criticism* he had published a book in which may be heard the first rumblings of that storm of 'theory' which crashes about the ears of university teachers of

English today. (The volume was one in a series of works called collectively *The International Library of Psychology, Philosophy and Scientific Method.*) With C. K. Ogden, his colleague at Magdalene College, Cambridge, he had collaborated in another book, grimly entitled *The Meaning of Meaning.* A pupil of his at the same college, William Empson, had just published (virtually from his cradle, one felt) *Seven Types of Ambiguity.* And Richards' *Practical Criticism* (1929) was one of the most useful books teachers of my own generation owned on shelf or desk.

But about *Practical Criticism* there was a point of delicacy with us at Leeds. One of the twelve poems it anatomizes (and in this instance unkindly) was from a collection of Wilfred Childe's called *Ivory Palaces.* It is a poem about clouds, and ends with the lines:

> O how the clouds this dying daylight crown
> With the tremendous triumph of tall towers!

Richards's harsh treatment of his poem was far from worrying Wilfred; far from disturbing that marvellous placidity. He was a poet. Richards was not. So that was that.

Nevertheless, and for the rest of us, the circumstance a little troubled the chatty green-room preliminaries to Richards's lecture. And certainly it was responsible for my own resounding *faux pas.* Presented to the great man, I expressed the hope that we weren't going to hear any more about 'The Windhover'. The background to this was simple. Gerard Manley Hopkins's astonishing poem was then all the go. Everybody was declaiming it and expatiating on it. Humbert Wolfe had been doing so, to more or less excruciating effect, only a few weeks previously. So what I was, in fact, saying to I. A. Richards was that we needn't fear anything more about this overexposed masterpiece from *him.* He turned the conversation at once, being far from minded to humiliate a gauche young man. And, of course, 'The Windhover' proved to be an early high-point in his lecture. He spoke the poem — and with exquisitely controlled gestures as he came to 'the rolling level underneath him steady air'. Richards had everything; he was a skilled rock-climber; he knew to within a fraction of an inch where his every finger was. And then a dreadful thing happened. Richards had got far into the poem. He had got to 'Buckle!' and we were waiting, breathless, to learn whether, in 'the fire that breaks from thee then', it was the ultimate or penultimate word on which he would let an accent fall, when a door opened and a very late-comer, a lady, entered the hall. Richards didn't (as Marcus Niebuhr Tod had used to do) go scurrying to find her a seat. But he did break off, remain silent and immobile for what seemed a full minute at least, and then start anew:

I caught this morning morning's minion . . .

From this lecture I hurried back to Willow Cottage and went to bed, feeling that never again could I face even the friendly Luffy. But many years later, when I told the story of my horrendous gaffe to William Empson, he was much amused. It took a great deal, he said, to disconcert Ivor Richards. For me, that hadn't been quite the point.

The third lecturer is T. S. Eliot. Like his Magi, he had made his journey at just the worst time of the year . . . the very dead of winter. Leeds was smothered in snow. Nevertheless, there was, of course, a very big turn-out to hear so distinguished a speaker. I made sure of a seat by arriving early. Here was the principal literary occasion of my five years in the place.

At first all went well. The hall was snug even if the lecturer was a shade chilly. But the hall was the one built in 1885, and its steam heating was probably still what had then been installed. The system wasn't very reliable; in fact it was notably short-breathed; in the bowels of the building there had to be a man stoking it up every half hour or thereabouts.

Eliot was soon to publish *After Strange Gods*, and as his discourse drew towards its close he advanced upon certain deeply-pondered and edifying considerations. Almost, it was a sermon. And it was now that the steam heating began to misbehave. The radiators, or perhaps the pipes connecting them, took to delivering what were distinguishable from pistol shots only by owning a certain clanking quality. Eliot, at his lectern, raised his voice a little, but appeared unperturbed. F. P. Wilson, sitting immediately behind him, was uneasy. I suppose he knew those pipes and radiators. He may also have known — what became generally known later — that the boiler-man was given to somnolence succeeding upon inebriety. The furnace, in fact, had been allowed to go out. And as the pipes cooled, the racket grew. Eliot talked on, but now detectably in the manner of one firmly resolved not to turn a hair. For a space the effect was inspiriting after a fashion; we were like troops steady in the face of a stiff assault by musketry. Or — a more trivial comparison — we were like a crowd at a fair, with people taking pot shots at a moving file of cardboard rabbits. But the pipes, at least, hadn't shot their bolt. Far from it. Quite abruptly, they changed what might be called their tune. What they now suggested was nothing of a martial or of a fair-ground character. Their new suggestion was — the word must be written — indelicate. Improper laughter at this made itself heard from some of the students present. The lecture ended. F. P. Wilson had prepared a neat little speech of thanks, in the course of which he gently touched in a small joke to the effect that Mr Eliot was a maker and breaker of literary reputations, like some powerful figure on the stock market. And at this commercial pleasantry, Mr Eliot ever so slightly elevated his eyebrows.

The evening wasn't over. There may have been an early but august dinner-party at the Wilsons, with the Black Baillies and persons of like kidney at the board. But the Wilsons felt that some of the rest of us should have a look-in, and as the lecturer was spending the night at their house, they had thought up a very small supper-party as a suitable conclusion to the affair. From the start I had misgivings about this, feeling that Eliot would have no wish to be further goggled at, and want simply to go to bed. But when I discovered that only Wilfred Childe and myself appeared to be involved, I was pleased and flattered beyond measure.

It was still snowing very hard. In the antique manner of those days, there were 'chains' on all four tyres of the Wilsons' car, but, even so, we slithered around a good deal on our way out to Headingley. The supper was sensible: brandy, together with a sandwich if one felt inclined to it. But now there was a ring at the door-bell, and a third bidden guest arrived. It was the Village Johnson.

In his autobiography, Alan Taylor's first mention of me avers that I 'specialized in witty descriptions'. There was, I suppose, wit of a sort in calling William Ker a Village Johnson — provided one remembered the Village Hampden in Gray's *Elegy*. Ker was an Inspector of Taxes, immensely well-read, and of a distinctly belligerent habit; he presided over a kind of informal literary club lunching once a week in a Leeds pub called the Cock and Bottle. Ker was a devout Catholic and therefore had a large family. He would be buried, he used to say, with a huge overdraft still round his neck — and meantime there was the recurrent problem of choosing suitable husbands for daughters. (I had vaguely thought of this as a virtually indecent habit more or less confined to France.) All this made Ker a worried man, and in this he resembled my friend Denis Binyon. But whereas Denis was diffident, Ker was unintermittently pugnacious. He was always a little alarming. What on this occasion — at so late an hour and from amid those obliterating snows — made him particularly so was that he brought with him a pair of enormous bedroom slippers. As he got out of his boots and galoshes and into these in Mrs Wilson's drawing-room, it was all too plain to me that he meant to 'have it out' (as he might have expressed it) with the eminent and metropolitan Mr Eliot.

William Ker was no fool, and he began by establishing his credentials — this by talking, knowledgeably and incisively, about those minor Elizabethan dramatists who had been Eliot's particular thing for some years. He then embarked upon theological discussion — as a Catholic requiring to know how our celebrated visitor thought to defend the absurd compromises of Anglo-Catholicism. Eliot, thus cornered in a provincial blizzard, quickly saw his only possible rôle. He was leisured, courteous, conversable, and distinguishably among friends of more than adequate calibre. I could think of him only as something straight out of Henry James.

But as hour succeeded upon hour, a sharper and sharper problem appeared: however was the evening, the night, to be brought to an end? The Wilsons themselves were plainly in a difficulty. They could scarcely turn us out of the house. Even to murmur to their house-guest that he must have had a tiring day would be a bit tricky. And Wilfred was, of course, hopeless. He wasn't asleep; it would have been unfair to think of him as being (in Stephen Leacock's phrase) in a state of Stodge or the Higher Indifference; he was simply and indefinitely his usual comfortable self, while being at the same time well aware of the comedy of the situation. So there was no help for it. I was by a long way the junior person present, but I had to make the move, all the same. Taking advantage of a brief pause in the talk, I rose, advanced upon Mrs Wilson, and enunciated my thanks and good-night. Mrs Wilson sweetly smiled. Eliot got to his feet instantly, shook hands with me, and then (very properly) at once sat down again. I suppose that my host saw me out, and I ploughed my way back to Willow Cottage. On the following day I asked Wilson when the little supper-party had ended. He murmured, 'Round about one o'clock.' Then he paused for a moment, and added, 'But, John, you did make an effort, didn't you?'

After that, I always addressed F. P. Wilson as 'David', which was his wife's name for him, and adopted by all his intimates. Percy Simpson, upon some similar consideration, was 'Philip' to Mrs Simpson, but that never caught on. Of a generation slightly senior to Wilson, he remained 'Simpson' when addressed, and 'Percy' when being referred to.

Of very minor interest compared with this of T. S. Eliot's lecture was a recurrent domestic affair at the university known as a *colloquium*. *Colloquia* happened at irregular intervals perhaps two or three times in a term, and each probably took its occasion from some member of the Faculty of Arts yielding to a strong feeling that he had something of urgency to communicate to the learned world at large. So there would be a cup of tea in a common-room, and then we would be called to order, and settle down to listen. I remember the Professor of French discoursing at length on the etymology of French fish names, a subject to which he had clearly devoted years of profound study. How had the Old High German *sturio* become *esturgeon*? There were, it seemed, endless conundrums of this kind. *Colloquia* worried Denis Binyon a good deal. Nurtured where he had been, he had a very sufficient sense of the virtue of pursuing knowledge for its own sake.

'But there must be limits, don't you think?' he would ask. 'All that, of course. But still! My uncle once told me to remember that all knowledge comes to us by the flicker of our mortal taper. What would you say?'

'There's a man somewhere in Montaigne, Denis, who'd taught himself to throw cumin seeds — or whatever the smallest conceivable seeds are — through the eye of a needle. He demonstrated his skill before some monarch, and was rewarded with a packet of cumin seeds.'

'Well, yes — I see.' Denis would be grievously puzzled by this flighty *non-sequitur*. 'But *esturgeon*, you know — and all that. And they say he just doesn't notice things. Lets his children go around with dirty finger-nails.'

'Never fear. *Tussis* will attack him.'

In full intellectual maturity — we were both getting on for the great age of twenty-five — Denis and I still found pleasure in such chatter, even when it took its prompting from a *colloquium*.

I recall a further occasion roughly of this sort happening in the same room as the *colloquia* — which must have been lent for the purpose, I imagine, to a local branch of the English Association. F. R. Leavis, already quite a name in the land, was coming to speak. A few days before this was due to happen, Wilson asked me whether I was going to turn up. I said I didn't think I was. Although I was a foundation subscriber to the recently established *Scrutiny*, the affair somehow didn't appeal to me. Wilson then said he would be greatly obliged if I could manage it. One of us ought to be present, and it so happened that Dr Leavis was 'personally offensive' to him. This was an utterly amazing thing for David Wilson to say. He was a man to whom you could talk for a year without hearing him utter an unkind word about anybody. And what the explanation was, I never discovered. But that Leavis was a rather tiresome man, I realized as soon as he began to speak. With a weary hand on brow, he explained to us the terrible burdens Cambridge imposed upon him. He stood, in fact, between the whole place and its perdition — so it had seemed to him that a journey to the yet deeper darkness of Leeds would positively be an evil dereliction of duty on his part. But then a further thought — virtually a revelation — had come to him, much as it had come to the Apostle Paul. 'Come into Macedonia, and help us.' Dr Leavis — we were made to feel — had experienced something like that. So here he was in Leeds. Of what he went on to say, I have no recollection. The reader must bear in mind that I am dealing with not very remarkable events occurring more than half a century ago.

Many years later, when I had become a don at Christ Church, I encountered Dr Leavis again — and this time not as a mere passive spectator. An invitation had come to me from an undergraduate literary society at Downing College, Cambridge, to go over and give a talk, spending the night in college. There was nothing out of the way in this; half a dozen such proposals would come to me in the course of a year, as I imagine they did to many of my colleagues. There was something slightly vexatious in the journeyings involved, but I generally went along, probably prompted by some general notion of academic amenity. At

Oxford such engagements were commonly regarded as entirely undergraduate affairs; the visitor was dined in a restaurant by a small committee of young people before putting on his turn. At Cambridge, which frequently has the edge over its sister university in these matters, it wasn't so. One began the evening as the guest of the senior members. It was at Downing, and after a good deal of shabby treatment by the University at large, that Dr Leavis had become a fellow in 1935, and it was thus that I found myself, as was obviously proper, dining beside him at high table. He was entirely charming — cordial rather than merely courteous — and we talked without effort throughout the meal. At its conclusion he was kind enough to lead me through the courts to the door of the junior combination room in which the meeting was to take place. At its threshold an appropriate youth was waiting to receive me. And at this point Dr Leavis shook hands with me and walked away. There were, after all, limits, and the great man wasn't going to listen to whatever nonsense I was about to talk. The meeting was entirely satisfactory. There was a good turn-out; I was heard with attention; an intelligent discussion succeeded. Yet, ever so faintly, what hung over the whole occasion was the sense of an agreeable prank successfully achieved. It was widely and correctly understood that the majority of the undergraduates whose studies Dr Leavis supervised were as devoted to him as were his colleagues in the *Scrutiny* venture. But was there some small dissident faction which had brought off an amusing *coup*? I was never to know.

Years later again, and in one of those metropolitan periodicals which he was in the habit of roundly condemning, Dr Leavis reviewed the principal academic labour I was ever to achieve. It was a smashing onslaught, and I was the more surprised to learn from it that *Eight Modern Writers* was 'in the Oxford tradition'. I had to read this bit twice before realizing that an aspersion was intended.

The most curious circumstance to occur during the five years of my academic apprenticeship at Leeds was the university's involvement, in a manner purely tangential and fortuitous, with the activities of T. J. Wise, perhaps the most successful, and certainly the most bizarre, literary forger of all time. Wise was the son of a commercial traveller, later turned tobacconist; as a young man he gained employment with a firm of essential oils merchants, with whom he made himself a prosperous career. But he was never a really wealthy man, and this makes his achievement all the more remarkable. Early a passionate devotee of poetry and of the collecting of books, he was equally precocious in the real task to which he had dedicated himself. He is said to have persuaded Robert Browning of the authenticity of a fabrication of his — Wise's — own: a supposed 'pre-first' edition of a work by the poet's wife. Browning died in 1889, and from this it may be inferred that Wise had perfected before he was thirty what was to remain to the end his prime method of deception. And he remained extremely pertinacious as a serious collector. Possessed of only moderate means as he was, he built up in what he called the Ashley Library what came to be widely regarded as the most important private collection of books in the country. I first heard the names 'Wise' and 'Ashley' frequently pronounced with husky awe by that severe and impeccable scholar, Percy Simpson. To be admitted to the Ashley Library, it appeared, was to establish oneself as ranking among the pre-eminent literary savants in England.

I don't know when this enterprising person made the acquaintance of Lord Brotherton. Brotherton was a Yorkshire ironmaster of great wealth, and perhaps ironmasters have occasionally to interest themselves in essential oils. However it may have been, Wise got hold of Brotherton and persuaded him to collect books. This in itself was an achievement, Brotherton being rather pronouncedly not a bookish man. It was also extremely useful. As a bibliophil, Wise was nothing if not a perfectionist. When a more nearly perfect copy of something came his way, he promptly parted with the less perfect copy he had put up with hitherto. It was probably in this fashion that a good many books came to be bought by Lord Brotherton.

But Wise, as well as providing books, provided a librarian. He had already set up a certain J. A. Symington (formerly a clerk in the essential oils concern) as an antiquarian bookseller; he now established him with Brotherton as Brotherton Librarian. Mr Symington was to be called that. He liked calling himself that. I remember seeing a letter of his in *The Times Literary Supplement* signed 'J. A. Symington: Brotherton Librarian'. It was rather as if he were writing from the Bodleian.

It must have been about halfway through my time at Leeds that there came the stupendous news that the Brotherton Collection was to be bequeathed to the University. Or not exactly that. A mere provincial institution was scarcely important enough for such a distinction. So the University was to hold the Collection 'in trust for the nation', and presumably to hold Mr Symington on the same terms. Then more, much more, followed.

To house the Brotherton Collection there was to be a Brotherton Library, within which, physically, the existing University Library would be subsumed. There was gossip to the effect that Lord Brotherton had made only one major stipulation to accompany this magnificent gift of bricks and mortar. The new building was to be circular, and its diameter was to be not less than that of the reading-room of the British Museum. Persons of ungenerous mind murmured that this was mega-lomania in the most literal sense of the term. There were others who, as the plans unfolded, noted with disapproval the striking disparity proposed between the material splendours which were to surround the Brotherton Librarian and the very modest accommodation proposed for the University's existing librarian, an austerely scholarly man who was an authority on Spanish-American literature.

This was the state of the case when the University's two professors of English, F. P. Wilson and a remarkable philologist called Bruce Dickins, were invited to Lord Brotherton's mansion outside Leeds to view the Brotherton Collection in its temporary quarters there. Wilson, who held strict Oxford views on who was whose colleague, asked me to go along with them. I was a good deal startled by this distinction. We were received by Mr Symington in a complex of stables and similar offices which had been converted for their temporary purpose regardless. (Only this colloquialism is adequate to evoke the makeshift splendours that had been contrived.) And there all the stuff was: from the more or less useless run of Shakespeare folios and quartos — items far beyond the purse of T. J. Wise — to important collections of manuscript and other material assembled on a regional Yorkshire basis.

Mr Symington's principal pride was his catalogue. This was assembled on an outsize card-index basis, which added to the due bibliographical information on each item appropriate literary-critical aperçus culled from diverse sources by Mr Symington himself. I seem to remember — but this may be only because I am a novelist — that some of these authoritative pronouncements were credited to Lord Brotherton. Confronted by this, David Wilson found a polite word to say now and then. Not so Bruce Dickins. In suggestion curiously boneless, Dickins was seldom if ever either motionless or mute. Rocking gently from one foot to the other, he would steadily emit low mooing noises, suggestive of some distant herd of cattle in urgent need of vaccimulgence. But now, and as if nothing in particular were going on or being said, he remarked that there were some very nice rugs around the place. This was no doubt true; the rugs were probably as choice as any to have come out of Persia; perhaps only the mosque at Ardebil could have matched the best of them. But if offence was intended by this inconsequence on Bruce Dickins's part, none was received. A generalized admiration for all things Brothertonian seemed entirely in order to Mr Symington.

The later history of the treasures over which Mr Symington presided was not altogether a happy one. Scholars asking for a rare book from the Brotherton Collection came to be told with surprising frequency that unfortunately it was on loan to some other scholar at a distant, virtually an inaccessible, corner of the globe. Considerable embarrassment attended the clearing up of this mystery.

Transitional

ON ANY SORT of professional front, I was far from being at this time a self-confident young man. I had, indeed, discovered that I could lecture fairly well, but there my aptitude for academic teaching seemed to stop off. We ran small seminars in the English Department, and they were sufficiently akin to tutorials proper to tell me that as a tutor I had a long way to go. I had to repel the thought that Percy Simpson was to blame here: I couldn't do the job adequately because it had never been adequately done to me (except, of course, for a month or two in the field of Political Economy). But in fact the fault lay with Great Creating Nature; I had been born without the right pedagogic baton in my knapsack. Not long ago, I discussed this with a former Christ Church pupil. Well, yes, he said. Yes. My conduct of tutorials had perhaps been more diffusely agreeable than specifically useful in the way of criticism. And it had been rather on the anecdotal side. Yes, distinctly that. And then this middle-aged man said something that took me by surprise. 'Concentration and suggestion,' he said. 'Concentration and suggestion, my dear Colvin, are what I aim at in my poetry.' So I had reminisced about Percy's eccentricities as a tutor when as a tutor I ought to have been clearing up a misconception about Spenser's use of allegory in *The Faerie Queene* or something of that sort. Thus — as Feste says — the whirligig of time brings in his revenges.

I had done another small job for Francis Meynell. I had written what may have been quite a lively brief life of Coleridge; but when it was turned down by both the Hogarth Press and a publisher then dealing in a big way with brief lives, I had chucked it in the waste-paper basket. I suspected that David Wilson was becoming a little anxious about me. He would remark that Sir John Suckling appeared to stand in need of editing — or, if not Suckling, then William Shenstone. John Florio had told me there was no road that way. Nor did I at all see myself as a critic. I had been taught that critics of any consequence were very rare cattle indeed.

Then something uncommonly strange happened. I was made aware — through what channel I have no recollection — of the presence in England of the Vice-Chancellor of the University of Adelaide (which was somewhere in Australia), together with a professor from the same place. They wanted me to go to lunch with them. Or, rather, they wanted my wife and myself so to do. The Vice-Chancellor, Sir William Mitchell, possessed, along with higher endowments, a substantial measure of practical sagacity, and he knew where the nub commonly lay in the sort of business he might find himself minded to transact with me.

So we went along. I found the money, that is to say, for a couple of return railway-tickets to London, and we lunched with these two learned men in their hotel. Sir Archibald Strong, I was told, had died the year before. Sir William gave the impression that I must know about Sir Archibald, who had been Jury Professor of English at Adelaide, and otherwise distinguished as well. And at this, I suppose I said the right thing.

'I'm afraid I haven't heard of him,' I said.

Sir William's accompanying professor (he was the Professor of Philosophy) gave some indication of disapproval at this. But Sir William himself had made up his mind. He set his table-napkin down on the table and suggested that we take coffee in his private room. Some ten minutes later (or so, in my recollection, it seems to have been) I was offered the late and distinguished Sir Archibald's job. But I mustn't hurry. *We* mustn't hurry. We must consider the proposal entirely at leisure, and then let him know whether or not I accepted it.

At this the Professor of Philosophy turned abruptly helpful. It would do no harm, he said, to look up sailings at once — and he did so in some relevant brochure produced from a pocket. A Blue Funnel steamer, the *Anchises*, looked about right. It was, among other things, a single-class affair: an advantageous way of travelling, on the whole. The professor pronounced the name of Aeneas's father as if it rhymed, or chimed, with 'cheeses'. This slightly startled me, and in Sir William it produced the only flicker of irritation I was ever to observe in him. But at once he had his own thought about the *Anchises*. Its sailing, in about three months' time, would be well after the end of the academic year at Leeds, so there would be ample leisure to make a little tour of the continent of Europe before setting out for Australia. We mightn't, after all, be seeing Florence and Delphi again in any very immediate future. But Sir William was quick to add that to regard Australia as in any way remote from England was entirely anachronistic. Nowadays one could fly from Adelaide to London in 48 hours (or whatever number of hours it then actually took). There was something slightly disingenuous in this, since Sir William Mitchell happened to be a very wealthy man. So I said — perhaps a shade shortly — that within the next couple of weeks my wife and I hoped to manage a few days in the Lake District.

Sir William pounced on that at once as a peculiarly felicitous circumstance. We could call on Darnley Naylor. He was an Englishman who had for long been Professor of Classics at Adelaide, but who had lately retired a little early and come home in order to undertake a translation of the complete poetry of Horace. Naylor would tell us all about the University of Adelaide, and about South Australia in general. His house was on the edge of Derwent Water.

So not very long afterwards we found ourselves being given tea by Professor Naylor. We had hit upon a notable day, since a first batch of proofs of his big undertaking had been delivered on him that morning. Treating us as friends at once, he read to us from these, although not at any oppressive length. Then he talked about South Australia, and of course much of what he said was news to us. In character it differed a good deal from the other Australian states, chiefly because it had been started bang off in the early 1830's as a fairly large-scale capitalist enterprise. Wealthy people in England had bought land in a big way; some had come out to live on it; others had stayed at home and simply watched its value grow. (I was to discover later that *The Times* had taken a majestically dark view of the venture, declaring its 'entire distrust of the whole character and tendency of such a project', and a 'hope that it may rather be strangled in the birth than live just long enough to spread disappointment and ruin'.)

Those who came out, Professor Naylor went on, had for the most part made the voyage on a ship called the *Buffalo*, and their descendants enjoyed a kind of *Mayflower* social status as a result. Nothing much had happened subsequently to disturb this order of things. There had been no convict settlements, no gold rushes, very little industry. If you didn't boast an ancestor on the *Buffalo* you would never be anybody very much in South Australia. There were about half a dozen ruling families.

This state of affairs, although mildly comical (Professor Naylor was unmistakably a well-bred Englishman), had in many ways proved advantageous. Take the University of Adelaide. Or take —what was much the same thing — William Mitchell. He was a simple Scottish boy, who had gone out when even younger than I was to be Professor of Philosophy and of several other things, including English Language and Literature. (When he had confessed to his near-contemporary, W. P. Ker, his total ignorance at least of the linguistic side of this last job, that future great scholar had given him a small book about Anglo-Saxon, and told him that if he read through this on the voyage out he would have no difficulty whatever in coping with that particular field of learning.) Arrived in Adelaide, Mitchell had fairly promptly married the principal heiress of the state and, thus established, had virtually taken charge of the still-infant university and built it up to a position of respectable quality and, in a sense, independence. The ruling families had taken on the job of dominating its governing body, and had paid up handsomely the while. A higher proportion of its revenues came from its own endowments than obtained in any other Australian university.

To this information I have to add that Mitchell remained an alert and productive philosopher — basically, I suppose, of the same neo-Hegelian order as his fellow-countryman, James Black Baillie. He published a weighty book called, I think, *The Structure and Growth of the Mind*. More remarkably, when in 1936 and far into his seventies he had read Alfred Ayer's *Language, Truth and Logic*, he had been heard to murmur amid the ruins (as they then seemed), 'I suppose it must all be true.'

In summary, Professor Naylor praised Adelaide and its university to us. It was a point that Australia had no Oxford or Cambridge to scoop the pool, so the cleverest young people born in the state came to their own university. One was seldom without two or three really able pupils. All in all, we'd find much to like if we went to Australia.

Having thus — metaphorically, so to speak — led us up the garden path, Darnley Naylor, on our taking leave of him, literally led us down it again. We paused at his front gate. Derwent Water lay before us. Due north, beyond Keswick, the peak of Skiddaw was just visible. Suddenly, Professor Naylor was agitated. For a moment, he touched each of us on the shoulder.

'But let nothing except penury,' he said, 'take you into exile. Goodbye.' And he turned and walked quickly back to his house.

So we went home to Leeds and considered whether penury it was. The point was curiously hard to determine. My university salary was to go up by £15 every second year: a disposition of things designed to encourage assistant lecturers to move on. My wife, a newly qualified doctor, earned useful guineas by visiting post-natal clinics all over the Yorkshire dales, but this entailed our having to employ the part-time services of a nurse for two sons, born within 363 days of each other. At the end of a week, we generally reckoned to be about fourpence in hand, and used to hold pleasurable debates on whether to expend this surplus on a block of chocolate or a Sunday newspaper. If at times there was rather more money around, this was because, at twenty-seven, I was still intermittently sponging on my father. And the future seemed bleak. Bruce Dickins, who specialized in disagreeable speeches, told me I'd never afford to send my sons to the sort of school I'd been to myself. Against all this was the fact that we were, in one way and another, making do; and that we were sufficiently high-spirited to get a good deal of fun out of it. My wife's instinct was for us not to give in (for that was what it came to). I, for my part, perhaps took too much thought for the morrow. Or for the next five years — for I declared it would be that. It proved to be for ten.

Measured by the flicker of one's mortal taper, ten years can seem incontestably a major effluxion of time. But time is tricky. Shakespeare's Rosalind knows that it 'travels in divers paces with divers persons': ambles, trots, gallops, stands still. It ambles on journeys at sea, and those who organize such journeys for pleasure are vigilant to provide constant shipboard diversion throughout the day and even far into the night. Not that really long voyages are nowadays very easy to achieve. The giant liners of yesterday still, indeed, plough the oceans, but it is on 'cruises' scurrying from one to another place of picturesque interest on *terra firma*. One has to crew on a nuclear submarine to achieve a really long spell at sea.

It still wasn't quite so in 1935. The Blue Funnel ships sailed to Australia by way of the Cape of Good Hope, and Cape Town appears to have been their only common port of call before reaching Fremantle. Until setting sail on the *Anchises*, my own longest journey by sea had been on a Yugoslavian steamer which I had boarded at Trieste and disembarked from at Spalato (now called Split). So the long haul across the South Indian Ocean — a matter of weeks rather than days, it seemed to be — was a new experience. I don't think we saw another ship. Flying fish were an event; dolphins a sensation. On our minute speck on the endless waters the prescriptive things went on: observing the captain and an officer making observations at noon; participating in a daily sweepstake on the distance covered on the preceding day; playing endless deck games; constantly accepting small bowls of soup; dressing religiously for dinner — a practice of almost none of us, I imagine, when at home. Several times a day a steward with a bugle went round the ship, summoning us to meals. He was invariably accompanied by our two toddlers: a spectacle occasioning much photographic activity on the part of our fellow passengers. Every morning another steward briskly summoned us to a bath in which a minuscule drop of the surrounding ocean had been hotted up for us. Amid all this, the omnipresent vastness had us increasingly in its grip. We'd had no notion that our comfortable but inconsiderable planet was the huge affair it was proving to be. Like the soul of Galsworthy in that epigram of Humbert Wolfe's, we went on, and on, and on — until, indeed, a small and unexpected thing happened.

Although I had visited the engine-room and listened to various explanations offered to me, I had no very precise idea of how the *Anchises* was propelled. But unceasingly, night and day, a faint pulsation could be felt, an insistent creaking heard. Then I woke up in my bunk one morning, and neither felt nor heard anything at all. The *Anchises*, as if it were a painted ship upon a painted ocean, as if it were Noah's ark plonked squarely down on Ararat, was immobile and silent around me. And — if momentarily only — it was as if *time* had stopped. No motion without time; no time without motion. Suddenly, I was bang up against the space-time continuum.

The *Anchises* remained stationary for several hours, and some casual explanation was given. There hadn't remotely been any sort of mishap. For some commonplace and familiar reason it had been desirable to stop the engines so that an adjustment could be made, and as a consequence we had glided to a halt on what happened to be a perfectly calm sea. The effect on me as of a timeless or eternal moment (which are one and the same thing) was thus in its occasion wholly trivial and unremarkable; and my only other experience of the kind I cannot remember as having had any precipitating cause at all. I believe it is an experience that comes to many individuals, but seldom other than very rarely.

I can recall only three glimpses of dry land during those six weeks at sea. The first was of the Canaries (or perhaps it was Madeira) visible through a porthole early one morning. It was in a blazing sunshine, and told me that, within half a dozen days, I had dropped clean out of any world I knew. The second glimpse, far on the port horizon, was of the hulk of Africa, a low, dark line under brilliant stars, armies of unalterable law. Of Cape Town I preserve no visual memory, other than of the *Anchises* itself, nocturnally smothered in coal dust as the vessel took on sufficient fuel to carry us over the ocean ahead. Most of the passengers, experienced or forewarned, had gone ashore for the night, thus escaping a mucky and vastly noisy performance. But in the morning the *Anchises* was spotless again. My third glimpse was of Australia itself: the seaboard, I imagine, to the north of Perth. What it presented was a thin line of scattered homesteads with nothing but a kind of sparse scrub behind them: dwellings low on the ground, suggestive of drift-wood washed up by a tide, ready to be washed away again. These, I told myself, were human habitations, tenuously established here during some phase of over-population in certain small and distant islands from which I myself happened to come; gallantly but forlornly awaiting engulfment by some *status quo ante* in which an almost empty continent would again be thinly roamed by obstinately primitive persons with sticks or bones through their noses.

Although this first impression was, of course, extravagant, something of it was to remain with me, and in retrospect seems arguable still. The aboriginal inhabitants of the continent, whencesoever they came, evolved for themselves a various, complex and bizarre culture the exploration of which has taxed to the full the energies of several generations of anthropologists. But it is everywhere a culture bearing the impress of a habitat harsh and hostile to an almost incredible degree. There has never been an aborigines' hamlet, never a little cluster of hovels, let alone the dim foreshadowings of a city. A wurley or gunyah, which is a small tent-like affair of mud and brushwood, might occasionally serve as shelter for a night or two for some minute group of these people, to whom good fortune had accorded the boon of thus briefly interrupting endless wanderings in search of the barest subsistence.

The inimical environment remains. Here and there great pasture-lands, sheep stations, have been won from it, but it is present still, and as if waiting to pounce. Consecutive seasons of drought will devastate whole regions for years; others, injudiciously overstocked, will become creeping dust bowls where nothing can grow. Only the big pastoralists can live securely on the land, able to weather a lustre of disasters — or a decade, if need be. The little chap, the cocky-farmer, is doomed in such an exigency, and has perhaps to accept a hireling's lot; if, on the other hand, he has luck and prospers, he may well make a timely retreat, like a prudent man from the gaming table, to live out his days in a suburban villa to which he has given the name Torestin or Dunromin or Wyewurk. And in becoming an urban man he has probably become a dweller almost within sound of an ocean. For the great Australian cities are, without exception, on a seaboard, and an astonishingly high proportion of the country's population is concentrated in or around them. It is almost as if people obscurely feel that they may become a boat people one day, and depart as they came. But, of course, it won't be so. Indeed, if like Dr Johnson before us, we survey mankind from China to Peru, we may well conclude that Western civilization bears a rather better chance of survival in the antipodes than in either Europe or the Americas.

Adelaide

PORT ADELAIDE IS eight miles from Adelaide itself, and its Outer Harbour is six miles beyond that, so that when the *Anchises* at length tied up at the end of our interminable voyage nothing much except mud flats met the view. There was, however, a large poster telling us that Bunyip Soap was guaranteed under the Pure Food Act. We were, of course, prepared for surprises, and this was the first. The second was the press, and for them we weren't prepared at all. There were four or five journalists, and although they were plainly friendly young men and women I 'interviewed' very badly — as I have consistently done on various occasions ever since. My wife was invited to pronounce on homes and gardens: topics by no means indifferent to her, but no more to be talked about than other domestic sanctities. Our children's nurse had come with us for the voyage and to settle us in; she was the daughter of a prominent Leeds industrialist; she insisted on wearing her uniform, but was quite clearly a friend rather than an employee. The reporters could make nothing of this social anomaly — except, I suspect, to accord Muriel a clear alpha as an attractive young woman. Then Sir William Mitchell's limousine appeared at the quayside, and we were whisked into Australia.

Adelaide itself I judged at once to be a most attractive city — and I had, after all, both Edinburgh and Oxford to compare it with. It had been 'laid out' in the later 1830's by a certain Colonel Light, a splendid character whose father had been master of an East Indiaman, and his mother a daughter of the Chief of Kedah in the Malay Peninsula. Colonel Light, as became a soldier, was constantly alert to hypothetical military situations, and in planning his city he gave much thought to defensive consider-ations, devising mile-wide parklands which would afford a field of fire against an advancing enemy. A hundred years on, these and the wide straight streets that could be commanded by a musketry were virtually unaltered. The buildings, it is true, were nothing much. The most impressive of them, the railway station, jostled the parliament building, and the original small university was tastelessly dominated by an enormous and largely useless Great Hall in the Gothic taste and of recent fabrication. But a city, after all, is something other than the sum of what has been piled up in it, and Adelaide immediately declared itself as gracious to the view.

I think the next thing that really struck me was the oranges. They turned up on the table in our boarding-house that evening. Six weeks on food out of cold storage may have sharpened our appreciation of them, but they struck me as such fruit as I had never tasted before. One could imagine them as having been guarded during their growth by the daughters of Hesperus. Although other — and, to us, more exotic — fruit abounded, the oranges remained a special case until, some years later, they simply disappeared. Quite suddenly, there wasn't an orange in the shops. Nor, making a special journey, could one have bought one straight off the tree. They had been acquired wholesale, and for several crops ahead, by the harbingers of those American forces who were on their way to give us a hand against the Nips.

But the realities of geopolitics in the Pacific region were in nobody's head in 1935. The aborigines were on the way out, and their second cousins the yellow men weren't allowed in. Australia was a white man's country. When a newspaper ran a story of a 'Wake up' nature, in which Australia was overrun by an Asiatic power with horrific consequences, it was widely judged to be a tasteless extravagance, and allowed to flop.

Our second day was spent at the seaside. We were sent, that is to say, to a suburb of Adelaide called Brighton, where it was judged that we might advantageously take a furnished house for the summer. Brighton has a lovely beach and a lovely sea. And as Australian urban culture is essentially a beach culture (it is in the surf that the young Australians become as demigods) we would thus arrive, in a sense, at the heart of things. This was, no doubt, Sir William Mitchell's idea, and it was in his car, again, that we made the expedition. But it was a plan conceived — as his plans were apt to be — from an unrealistic economic elevation. Such houses as were available at short notice and within a reasonable price range, were ramshackle, dirty, miserably equipped, and inhabited by thousands of blowflies and mosquitoes. Firmly, we sounded a retreat.

On the next day again, I was taken by the Registrar of the university to call on the manager of the Bank of Adelaide for the purpose of transferring my 'funds' from England to Australia. When the sum involved was revealed as in the region of £15 the manager, of course, didn't bat an eyelid. But the Registrar, an elderly man called Eardley, with whom I had found myself instantly at home, joined in my own amusement at the situation. It had, of course, its serious side. I was to shed fairly rapidly any notion that I was going to be rather well off in Adelaide as compared with those Leeds days behind me. My salary was, I think, identical with that of the other professors, age or seniority bringing no increments. But there were few, I came to suspect, who didn't have something under the bed, or at least who didn't quietly pursue a sideline — owning, it might be, a market garden or a pie shop. It was a problem to be thought about, but which in fact solved itself without much thinking. The emptiness of the poet's purse is, rightly regarded, of no less dignity that are his laurels. But fate has never permitted me more than an occasional glimpse of it.

We rented a pleasant little furnished house in an inner suburb, but it soon became (we thought) too hot to hold us. It was only early summer, yet the heat was already astounding. There was, however, a resource open to us. Immediately behind Adelaide is a line of hills known somewhat grandly as the Mount Lofty Ranges. Mount Lofty itself (from which there is a magnificent view over the city at night) stands at 2,334 ft, and round about it are lesser hilly regions throughout which temperatures are considerably lower than on the plain. In one of these, called Blackwood, we found to let a house in which we were very lucky indeed. It was essentially a modest dwelling, but had one feature commonly found only in much older and more imposing mansions. The lower storey was in part dug into steeply sloping ground, so that there was a small range of rooms open at the front to light and air while being at the same time virtually subterraneous. The effect of this on the thermometer was quite astonishing. I sat in a little room much as I might have done in Leeds, and tapped out *Hamlet, Revenge!*

A couple of years later, because of schooling and for some other reasons — including, perhaps, having become seasoned to the South Australian climate in general — we moved down into Adelaide again. But we were never to own a house there, or even to settle in a rented one for a substantial spell of years. Not including holiday accommodation, we drifted through six such houses — or seven including much the nicest of them, which was several times lent to us by its owner, a much-travelled Australian lady called Kilmeny Symon, whom I had once chanced to meet at a party in London, and who was to be very positively our good angel through all our Adelaide days.

One of the first things I had to try to grasp in Adelaide was the concept of the Leading Citizen, which was constantly invoked in the local press. What advanced a man to this distinction remained a little obscure to me. That few, if any, of my new colleagues were leading citizens appeared right and proper, and was indeed among the more encouraging of my early discoveries. Scholars, I believed, had no business in the market-place, and little even in government. Later, indeed, I was to come to feel a certain dimness as apt to characterize those Australians who followed academic pursuits. If in that part of the world you were a notably clever boy, the last thing you were likely to become was a professor. Of course there were exceptions to this rule. Adelaide University itself had during its short history launched on their career several physicians and physicists of eminence. But, in general, the proposition held.

My predecessor in the Jury Chair, Sir Archibald Strong, appeared to have been a somewhat protean character, pertinaciously and successfully combining the rôles of professor and civic somebody. Almost, he seemed to have been the university's public-relations man; and this established association of job with job was, for a time, a little to devolve on me. I was quite comically unfit for anything of the kind. For one thing, I was at least fifteen years younger than any of the other professors in my faculty, and Australians in general have no taste for a *Wunderkind*. For another, I was a provincial dropped in among colonials. With anything done as it wasn't done in Oxford (or, at the least, Leeds) I felt there must be something seriously amiss. But if I was thus in some danger of intellectual arrogance I was diffident as well. So I disliked having to turn up at things in any sort of representative character.

I recall one such recurrently irksome requirement. It was having to attend amateur theatrical occasions. I was (and remain) much too inhibited a character to engage in anything of the sort myself;

and this, I think, was also true of my wife. But there were several dramatic societies in Adelaide, and during long seasons their entirely blameless activities happened two or three times a week. There was a single purpose-built — and large — theatre in the city, but the amateurs performed in various public halls which tended to be either uncomfortably chilly or (more commonly) unbearably hot. We had to go to the first night of all these affairs. It would have given offence not to do so, and we were determined never to offend. On this last point I am in no doubt whatever — a fact which renders the odder and weirder the following sad little story.

One of these dramatic societies was socially superior to the others, and very conscious of the fact. It liked to put on sub-Oscar-Wilde plays of high life such as were then being written by Frederick Lonsdale. The élite of Adelaide, that is to say, were fond of dressing up as earls and countesses, as Lord John and Lady Jane, and appropriately comporting themselves on the stage. If little could have been more boring, nothing could have been more harmless and innocent.

Obviously because of that representative character, I found myself a member of the managing committee of this society, and there somehow came a meeting at which commendatory re-marks on some particular production were required of me. As I recall the incident, my appreciation was insisted upon. I had been challenged, and had to speak, conscious that there was a totally unfamiliar whiff of something like xenophobia in the air. So I said that the performance had reminded me of Cardinal Newman's description of the night-life of Birmingham as an uncouth imitation of polished ungodliness. I really believed that my borrowing of this undeniably elegant little anecdote (which I had probably had from Percy Simpson at the end of one of his tutorials) would be received as an agreeable if slightly astringent contribution to the discussion in hand.

But now I read through this last paragraph, and doubt assails my elderly and unreliable memory. Did I actually *utter* that graceless quip, or did I only *think* of it? Yet even if the latter supposition be true, it was certainly not an instance of *l'esprit de l'escalier*. That the thought was instant — that it did as I sat at that table come into my head — I am as sure as a man can reasonably be of any small event 50 years behind him. And it suggests that, intermittently at least, I found myself in a somewhat trigger-happy state, and not shaping up too well as an inoffensive pommy.

Of the facts of another small *contretemps* in Adelaide I am again in some doubt. Essentially it was a Michael Innes *contretemps*, arising from the fact that in *Hamlet, Revenge!* I had called a butler Bagot — having taken the name quite inconsequently, I think, from Shakespeare's *King Richard II*, where it occurs in a clump along with Bushy and Green. But — inexcusably, indeed — I had quite forgotten that, here in Adelaide at somebody's hospital luncheon table, I had met a Mr Bagot, a leading architect who was no doubt a leading citizen as well. He was also an admirer of Mussolini — under whom, he explained, Italian trains had begun to run on time. Believing, as I did, that no liberal-minded Englishman ought to visit this bombastic dictator's Italy, and aware that I had myself breached this injunction only to the extent of spending a single night in Trieste, I had — momentarily, at least — rather taken against Adelaide's Mr Bagot. So is it possible that, when I named my butler as I did, some unconscious petty malignity was at work in me? Mr Bagot certainly thought there had been nothing unconscious in question. I had deliberately insulted him, and he wrote a letter to me to that effect. His father, he said, had employed a handyman called Stewart. But he had never known a menial Bagot.

That this comical explosion generated a certain aftermath of awkwardness cannot be denied, and it was an awkwardness augmented by the restricted dimensions of the Adelaide community. Everybody who wore a tie as well as a collar tended to be aware of the identity of everybody else thus superfluously accoutred. I found myself quite frequently in the same company as Mr Bagot, and with a kindred frequency we passed one another in the street. Mr Bagot, moreover, was the university's architect, and he made a meticulous annual inspection of every corner of the place. This included a visit to my own room, which was in fact a small disused laboratory roughly adapted to humane purposes, and containing a number of sinks and taps which had to be peered at. Mr Bagot and I would exchange stiff bows on these occasions, and as the years went by I came to wonder more and more that our little affair of honour hadn't ended on a duelling-ground.

It ended, as it turned out, rather differently. In my very last week in Australia, prompted by my wife's insistence that the manner of our departure should be as becoming as might be, I had accepted for the two of us an invitation to a polite affair run by Adelaide ladies, at which tea and sandwiches were followed by a speech or paper from a principal guest. The guest on this occasion turned out to be Mr Bagot. He was on again about Italy — although this time it wasn't Mussolini but the country's *giardini tagliati*. Never having been in Italy, I had never seen a *giardino tagliato*, but I realized from the start that Mr Bagot thoroughly knew what he was talking about. He grew eloquent over it, and towards the close his eloquence was visibly affecting him. He had to produce a pocket handkerchief. At this my own propensity to something like tears must have been remembered by my wife, who murmured to me, 'Off you go.' So I got to my feet, made my way to Mr Bagot, and thanked him for the pleasure his paper had afforded me. He instantly shook hands, and bade me *bon voyage*.

It was, perhaps, about halfway through my time in Adelaide that there occurred the curious Ern Malley affair, and the resultant discomfiture of a pupil of mine called Max Harris. I am happy to know that Mr Harris became an established figure in the Australian literary world, but at the time at which the episode occurred he occupied a somewhat exposed position as the young poet and propagandist of an *avant-garde* that didn't very obviously exist. He edited a periodical called *Angry Penguins* — the title coming from a line of his verse which ran, if I remember rightly:

> Drunks, those angry penguins of the night . . .

To my own mind, at least, the best thing about *Angry Penguins* was a pictorial cover provided by another young man — one destined, as it happened, to wider fame, Sidney Nolan. Harris in those early days perhaps rendered a slightly bumptious impression, and this may have prompted two of his fellow poets, resident in a neighbouring state, to take him down a peg. To this end they invented Ern Malley, a youth late deceased in beggary or thereabouts, who had left a sister — or perhaps mother — aware of two things: that Ern had been a queer lad, always scribbling poems and hiding them away in drawers, and that Mr Harris, as the acknowledged prime littérateur of Australia, was the man to contact about this strange family phenomenon. For all this, Harris fell in a big way. He possessed himself of the Ern Malley poems, and printed them in a special issue of *Angry Penguins*, together with much material of a biographical, critical, and eulogistic nature. The perpetrators of the hoax then blew the gaff. They had fudged up the poems in a pub: that sort of thing.

Harris, faced with disaster, behaved stoutly. Having some command of money at the time, he cabled the entire Malley *corpus* to Herbert Read in England, and required his comment. Read, an eminently serious if readily impressionable man, did his stuff — declaring, we were told, that the mockers had mysteriously themselves been mocked. In that pub, although they didn't know it, the sacred coal had been at their lips. But as few in Adelaide (my own pupils apart) had heard of Herbert Read, there was continued confident laughter over the late Ern Malley. I didn't myself feel at all that way inclined. In our age, as in most others, poets have a hard row to hoe, and two of them ought not to gang up against a third. There had been, it seemed to me, a kind of *trahison des clercs* in the joke.

And the joke had a sequel. Harris was down, and the powers that then were in Adelaide decided that here was the time to take a smack at him. He had undoubtedly done things to annoy. For example, he had committed to print the statement that an Adelaide lady of the substantial class was a *demi-mondaine*. By this he meant to say that the lady hovered between fashionable and literary circles. Harris, never, I fear, having taken time off to acquire much in the way of an education, was totally unaware that the term commonly implies a doubtful repute of a specific sort. He was called upon to apologize, which I believe he promptly did, and there the Harris-baiting ought to have ended. On the strength, however, of various pieces appearing in *Angry Penguins* he was called into court and charged with uttering obscene libels. And I was warned off.

By this I mean that I was summoned one day to Mr Eardley's office, and there found a judge of the South Australian High Court. The judge was making it his business to advise me, 'most strongly', in no circumstances willingly to come forward with evidence in Mr Harris's favour. Only if served with a subpoena ought I to have anything to do with the matter.

I can see now, 50 years on, that the man had a point. In any court's witness-box, and after a fashion, my voice would be the voice of the University of Adelaide, and it would be speaking in defence of a good deal of sorry stuff. But there was the awkward fact that I didn't see the sorry stuff as properly to be called obscene libel. So I was obliged to tell the judge that I'd have to consult my own mind on the matter, and at that I withdrew. Whether or not he was outraged, I don't know. And in the issue I accepted the request of Harris's solicitor to give evidence on the accused man's behalf, and thus had to spend half an hour in a witness-box, having bits and pieces out of *Angry Penguins* read to me, and saying No, it might be coarse and crude and so on, but it wasn't obscene. Havering thus, I was heard with oppressive respect. Then Max Harris was found guilty, and fined some nominal sum. It has occurred to me since that I was perhaps the first person to be permitted to give 'expert' evidence in any British court on the quality of a literary work. (It was long before the *Lady Chatterley's Lover* affair. My part in *that* was to be singularly inglorious. I was vetted as a possible witness for Connie Chatterley, and very justly turned down.)

Later than all this, I had a brush with the yet higher judiciary. The Chief Justice, a man called Sir George Murray, who was also Lieutenant-Governor of South Australia and Chancellor of the University as well, occasionally presided, I imagine, over our governing council, but I remember only one occasion on which he took the chair at a meeting of a much less important body, the education committee. This was just the professors. (Traffic was allowed past the windows when the education committee was meeting, but banned when the meeting was of council.) But there Sir George was, and disposed to be extremely grave. Within the university, it seemed, subversion was rearing its ugly head. Young people with very undesirable opinions and attitudes were being freely admitted merely if they passed the necessary examinations. So requiring testimony by a responsible citizen as to a boy's or girl's right thinking might be a good idea. At the least, matriculation should be granted to a candidate only if he or she were prepared to make a solemn pledge to be a model in this regard. Just what form this would take didn't appear. Perhaps our undergraduates were to declare themselves well affected to the Crown, or something of that sort.

When Sir George had finished nobody seemed disposed to speak, although there were a few nods and murmurs of approval round the table. So I spoke up myself, saying that the proposal surely took us a little away from the idea of a university, which was of a home for the intellect and open-mindedness in general. Of course, as a junior person I ought not to have spoken at all, and I had certainly gone trigger-happy again. Even so, I am sure I was quite temperate and quite brief. Before I had finished, however, Sir George Murray got up and walked from the room.

The interesting thing about this tremendous rebuke is that it had positively no aftermath whatever. At the meeting, I suppose Sir William Mitchell moved into the chair, and some necessary business was transacted. And thereafter, nobody had anything to say about the matter. It wasn't quite that my colleagues were charitably ignoring a *faux pas* on my part, nor, contrastingly, that they were diffident of offering a supportive word. It was unfortunate that I had offended the Chancellor, but not of much interest or consequence.

Australians have great power of disregarding speculative issues, particularly if these tend to threaten the sovereign duty of any group to remain 'cobbers' together.

But I must not linger on this antagonistic note. Adelaide, including its university, had much to offer. Academically we were a relatively small concern, existing in considerable isolation, and I was without colleagues affording me any stimulus in my own field. But quite as important as his colleagues to a university teacher are his pupils — and Darnley Naylor had spoken truly when he said that in this regard I'd be well provided for. I was never without first-class young minds around me; and in this, of course, I cannot have been exceptional. Indeed, I came to feel of the place as a whole that it was the best students rather than their professors and lecturers who set its academic standards.

Professionally, my wife's experience was a little odd. There existed full reciprocity between Australia and the United Kingdom in point of medical qualifications, and she expected in one way or another to make herself useful as a doctor. Inquiry, however, elicited the extraordinary information (or influential opinion) that it would be invidious for the wife of a professor of the university to accept medical employment necessarily of a junior character. But she would be welcomed at once on the committee of the Mothers' and Babies' Health Association, which was composed entirely of ladies in a socially prominent position in the community. This nonsense annoyed us both, but my wife wisely closed with the proposition at once. It resulted in her seeing a good deal more of South Australia than I did, since eventually she was asked to go on a tour of inspection of the

Association's branches in the remoter areas of the State — an experience that left her with a high opinion of Australian women 'out back'.

With the war, her position changed radically. Australia's male doctors seemed to depart for it almost to a man, with the result that the services of women doctors were at a premium. In no time my wife found herself virtually running Adelaide's Children's Hospital, and together with another Englishwoman running South Australia's blood bank as well. She became a captain in the military forces of the Commonwealth at about the same time that I became a private in them. In my own case — apart from a medical examination and the taking of some sort of oath — it was an empty form; in hers it meant two arduous jobs, along with five young children at home.

When I try to think back to Australia during the years of war I become very conscious of the tricks of memory. I am writing, after all, of a period of just short of half a century ago, and of actions most of which came to us as reports from another hemisphere. 'This country and Germany are now at war.' Of the tone of voice in which Neville Chamberlain's statement came to me over the wireless on 3 September 1939 I have the most precise recollection. But the setting of this occasion as I now see it is perplexing and improbable: I am sitting in a car which, surely, we no longer possessed, in the garage of a house which, surely, we weren't then living in, and listening to a radio I have no other memory of owning.

On the events of June 1940 my imagination has also been at play. We had decided that our eldest son should go to a boarding-school near Melbourne (it proved to be a short-lived experiment) and had driven him over from Adelaide, taking two or three days for the trip. Returning, we spent a cold winter night in a primitive hotel in some hilly country called the Grampians. We got up and went out early, hoping that a brisk tramp would warm us up a little. We met a woman with a cow. She told us of having just heard that the Germans had taken Boulogne.

Later that day — or was it the day before? — we drove through an interminable Australian emptiness (but once there was a line of kangaroos on the horizon) and came upon a pub. Several men were lounging against its veranda-posts, and a loud-speaker hitched to the top of one of these posts was blaring something without much gaining their interest or attention. We drew up for a few moments to hear what was being broadcast. It was a news-bulletin announcing that General Gamelin had ordered the armies of France to stand and fight to the death. So we went on our way, knowing that what was being called the Battle of France must have ended in total defeat.

The hard core of this experience was undoubtedly what I here describe. But to what extent has my imagination since embroidered on it? Australian friends have proved sceptical about all that vastness of mere scrub on any route from Melbourne to Adelaide. (They even doubt the kangaroos.) And how could that pub have come into existence, or how have survived, in the middle of a terrain dispeopled from horizon to horizon? The truth of the matter may lurk in something else I seem to remember. Not only is there all that of indifferent or hostile vacancy in my picture; not only is the pub unbelievably ugly and ramshackle and impermanent, and the lounging men of a piece with it. I also see, sparsely scattered around, the skeletons or decaying carcasses of what are evidently sheep. So that is my final picture: a loud-speaker bellowing out the fall of France to dejected drinkers and dead animals in an alien hemisphere. Over the years, the powerful and authentic art of Sidney Nolan has got to work on my picture.

Almost exactly twelve months later, something like that encounter with the woman with the cow repeated itself. We were living once more in the hills above Adelaide: again in a rented house, but now with our own furniture. (It was furniture picked up at cheap auction-sales, but giving us an inordinate pleasure, all the same.) Our situation was comfortably isolated, with no other dwelling visible. Our nearest neighbour, just over the brow of a hill, was a cocky-farmer whom I would visit early every morning to collect milk. And one morning at the end of June he gave me news he had just heard on the air. Hitler had invaded Russia. I realized at once that this was horrible news, since it presaged almost certain slaughter on a scale the war had hitherto not produced. But I also wondered whether Hitler had read *War and Peace*.

We were ourselves without a wireless (which was still the current word for a radio) throughout the second half of 1941: a fact surely revealing a lack of urgency in our receiving news about the war. Perhaps I had more confidence in Adelaide's newspaper, the *Advertiser*, than in the Australian Broadcasting Commission. But in the first week of December I did, for some reason, buy a set and bring it home. I plugged it in, switched it on, and nothing happened. I said, 'It doesn't work' — having forgotten that (in those days) such machines took some seconds to warm up. It duly warmed up, and what came from it was a news-flash to the effect that the Japanese had launched a surprise attack on a place called Pearl Harbor in Hawaii, and had inflicted catastrophic damage on the American Pacific Fleet.

There must, I suppose, have been in the world a great many people who happened to switch on wireless sets just in time to hear that. But the small *coup de théâtre* which chance had brought off in that little house in the middle of South Australian scrub I rate as the oddest thing that ever happened to me.

With ominous speed — in fact three days later — the Japanese sank the *Prince of Wales* and the *Repulse,* and a day after that again they had taken Guam. There were formal declarations of war: Britain and the United States against Japan almost before the smoke had cleared from Pearl Harbor; Germany and Italy against the United States on 11 December. A week after that, Hitler had assumed command of the German army. Hitler, of course, was done for, and Hirohito with him: no clear-headed person, aware of the awesome might of America, could have been in doubt about that. But what of Australia meanwhile? Hong Kong fell on 25 December, and Singapore three weeks later. Suddenly, the war was on our doorstep. I don't think there was much panic, nor even as much anxiety as there might well have been, particularly as a good part of Australia's young manhood was in the deserts of North Africa. But the prime minister, John Curtin, had ordered these forces home — turning down a hazardous plan by Winston Churchill to pitch them into Burma on the Japanese flank. So they would soon be defending their own country, which it was generally felt they were very well able to do. I myself never doubted their courage, but I did calculate their numbers, and I can recall my considerable relief when I saw my first American airman in an Adelaide street.

And soon there was General MacArthur. From the very northernmost tip of the Philippines, we were told, and on the order of his President, he had set out in a speedboat that never stopped until it reached Darwin, 2,000 miles away. Then somehow he had got to Alice Springs, and by the time he reached Adelaide 36 hours later he had mysteriously accreted around him a staff that taxed the entire rolling stock in that part of Australia. Behind him, 70,000 American troops were being made captive by the Japanese. But of that there was nothing to be said but *c'est la guerre.*

Curtin proved to have been right; it was the Australians who held on to a corner of New Guinea until, island by island, the Americans achieved control of the Pacific. Some of my pupils lost their lives in defending Port Moresby. One who survived apologized to me for having had to abandon to the jungle my six-volume *Everyman* edition of Gibbon's *Decline and Fall of the Roman Empire*. It had been in a sudden exigency of combat.

We left Australia on 1 December 1945 as seven of the ten passengers on board a cargo steamer called the *Fremantle*. My pupils — most of them girls at that date — presented me with the four volumes of *The Cambridge Bibliography of English Literature*, and a group of them came to the Outer Harbour to wave us off. Whether there was still a hoarding proclaiming the edibility of an excellent soap, I don't know. What lay ahead of us had its problematic aspects, and what we were leaving had been agreeable in many ways — not least in point of numerous friendships which were to bring us many visits from Adelaide people in the years ahead. Nevertheless, our predominant feelings as we set sail were of relief and liberation. We were to be free of a persistent home-sickness which at times had threatened to deepen into a nostalgia proper.

Let nothing except penury take you into exile.

Michael Innes (1) Making a Start

ALAN TAYLOR SAYS in *A Personal History* that during our years at Oriel I laughed at his 'excessive reading of detective stories'. If this was so, it was certainly a matter of the pot laughing at the kettle. In a list of books read during that time I find dozens of detective stories. And both in my later years at school and my five years in Leeds I certainly read a great many more. Indeed, it was when the thought came to me that in something like the time I habitually spent reading detective stories I might well be able myself to write one that Michael Innes was, as it were, born.

There was an element of muddle in this idea that takes a little clearing up. The detective story, at least during the period often spoken of as its 'golden age', called for much concentration during effective perusal. The reader was challenged to reach the truth of the matter in hand through a vigilant attention to minutiae much as a scholar is in certain exacting spheres of criticism; and there are plenty of scholars who enjoy directing upon a diversion the same sort of vigilance and severity that they habitually employ when at work. This wasn't at all my own attitude, and I am inclined to think that my pleasure in reading all those Agatha Christies and Ellery Queens long ago was lurkingly the pleasure of allowing myself to be lazy and cheat; to accept a comfortable bafflement as the story went on; and to finish the book with a sense that it had all been amazingly clever, and in places quite amusing as well.

When I began to write, or plan, *Death at the President's Lodging* (destined to be called *Seven Suspects* in the United States) I found, needless to say, that any such attitude wouldn't do. And I did buckle down at once. Taking the book from the shelf and re-reading it now for the first time since its composition (an experience strange in itself), I am chiefly struck by the sheer hard work that must have gone to slogging out an orthodox and extremely intricate plot. There are other elements designed to have a different appeal: dons talk donnishly, and undergraduates are routinely high-spirited. But the nub of the thing is the clues and where they lead to — and it is into a maze that actually concretizes itself (or burgeons) into a real maze at one point.

I find myself wondering when I began such a complex artefact and when I finished it: just how long it took to write. But, first, why a detective story at all? Why not an ordinary novel?

The answer to this preliminary question is simple. I was an immature student of literature, who had been living an awed existence amid its major monuments for quite some time. Proper novels seemed to me very serious affairs, legitimately to be attempted only by people of deep experience and keen perceptions of and into what was coming to be called the human situation. In these qualifications I seemed to be singularly lacking. Apart from some notable strokes of good fortune, nothing whatever had happened to me from the cradle onwards — or nothing which a rather inhibited young man would have cared to draw upon for fiction. *South Wind, Crome Yellow, Decline and Fall* were in regions as inaccessible as *Wuthering Heights* and *Moby Dick*. But detective stories were in a different category, belonging with a purely speculative scheme of things. They were also (and this must have been a factor with me) variously respectable. In one class of polite society writing detective stories had superseded writing ghost stories as an acceptable relaxation. Thus Cyril Alington when Headmaster of Eton had taken to producing the former while his senior, M. R. James, the Provost, was still turning out the latter. ('The Provost writes ghost stories and the Headmaster silly novels,' declared Oscar Browning, long since banished from the antique towers and pleasing shade.) I had myself discussed detective stories with luminaries of the magnitude of Ronald Knox and (on that snowy night) T. S. Eliot. J. C. Masterman, a Christ Church don who was presently to become Provost of Worcester College, and during the Second World War a supereminent cryptographer, had recently published *An Oxford Tragedy*. So to produce a detective story myself would not be wildly aberrant from an academic point of view. That it might in some slight degree be positively advantageous, somewhere prompting the thought that the fellow seemed competent in one thing as well as another: this was a persuasion that I was too inexperienced to entertain.

Alexander Pope somewhere makes fun of untalented persons who tumble into print 'constrained by hunger and request of friends'. I doubt whether anybody so much as hinted to me that I should write any sort of fiction. Hunger was another matter: it certainly came in. My children didn't yet (or, indeed, ever), in Hilaire Belloc's phrase, 'howl for pearls and caviare'. But things were, as I have indicated, pretty tight before I went to Australia; and it is my guess that at some date early in 1935 I began to write a detective story with the notion of its bringing in a little pocket-money. But, if this be so, it was almost at once put aside — partly by the distractions of the impending departure to the antipodes, and partly by a mass of School Certificate examining, which offered a more immediate and less speculative small cheque. Then, during the six weeks of the voyage to Adelaide, I took up the story again, and finished it. Arrived at journey's end, I had only to tap out a fair-copy on my typewriter, and pack it off to a publisher.

This version of the fabricating of *Death at the President's Lodging* doesn't quite stand up to my recent reading of it, and I now think it probable that I altered a good deal as I went along, elaborating and attempting to clarify the story. Even so, the completed text was fairly rapidly *en route* to England, and Mr Gollancz had it in the bookshops within a year of my having set sail from Liverpool.

Was this fairly rapid execution of a complex yarn a product of my new professorial status, and of self-confidence restored, or did it result from the sort of feeling that must have been experienced by the unfortunate nobleman in Belloc's poem who is sent out to govern New South Wales? I don't really know. But one factor operative here was my having arrived in Adelaide almost at the end of the university's academic year, and Sir William Mitchell's insistence that I should in no wise take up my new job until I had acclimatized myself in near-idleness to the long, hot Australian summer in which the universities wisely site their major vacation. I had, in fact, plenty of time in which to incubate that home-sickness. While tinkering with *Death at the President's Lodging* I was inhabiting in retrospect an English institution I believed myself to know very well; in its immediate successor in the Michael Innes canon, *Hamlet, Revenge!*, I was similarly, if contrastingly, prowling an English ducal dwelling of which I had no first-hand knowledge at all; and this was to be followed by *Lament for a Maker*, a heavily nostalgic Stevensonian story, set in Scotland and drawing upon the sort of people I came from. Ahead of that, again, stretched a series of eight romances, all written in Australia, six of which were set in England or Scotland. Of the two remaining, *Appleby on Ararat* opens on the sun-deck café of a liner when the café, through an incident of war, has been set floating upside-down on the Pacific Ocean with its occupants unharmed and scarcely disconcerted; while *The Daffodil Affair* concerns a lavishly paranormal colony on the upper reaches of what may be the river Paraná in Argentina (a sufficiently remote region of the globe to which my father, surprisingly, had once penetrated). These two extravaganzas, incidentally, are my principal attempts to bring a little fantasy and fun into the detective story. But the impulse has always been present with me, and has justly earned for me Mr Julian Symons's label as a *farceur* in the kind.

Detective stories are purely recreational reading, after all, and needn't scorn the ambition to amuse as well as puzzle.

Belfast

THE RESCUE OPERATION restoring me to my own hemisphere
was mounted by David Wilson, who was shortly to become
Merton Professor of English Literature at Oxford; and was to a
modest extent eked out by efforts of my own. Journals had
accepted a couple of papers into the fabricating of which I had put
a good deal of effort. Through several hot Australian summers I
had sat in a large steel box called a carrel in the basement of
Adelaide University's Barr Smith Library, and there written a
book called *Character and Motive in Shakespeare*: it had been seen
and approved by competent persons, but wasn't yet in print.
From a man just short of forty, this wasn't much. And on the
debit side of the ledger also — for so I conceived it — were all
those detective stories. It still didn't occur to me that, if they were
satisfactory in their kind, such things might earn the favourable
regard of the good and the great in academic life. Only many
years later did I learn — from the *Proceedings of the British Academy*
— that Sir Walter Greg, the most eminent Shakespeare scholar of
the time, had read *Hamlet, Revenge!* again and again, submitting it
to 'the same kind of scrutiny he gave to the variants in the first
quarto of *King Lear*'.

I suspect that I had another supporter in David Nichol Smith,
the incumbent Merton Professor, who had been one of my
examiners back in 1928, and who seemed to think of me as a
meritorious Scot. This David had had a brother, Gregory Nichol
Smith, who had been Librarian of the Queen's University in
Belfast, and himself variously distinguished as a scholar. These
facts combined to get me a lectureship at Queen's at very short
notice indeed. And this appointment established in turn an
adequate claim for an early passage home.

It had somehow been intimated to me that the English Department at Queen's had gone uncommonly drowsy and stood in
need of arousal. This certainly proved to be true. The Professor

of English, F. W. Baxter, was the nearest thing to a human dormouse ever to come my way — although, indeed, at Queen's he seemed to have numerous runners-up on the academic staff as a whole. But he was also a marvellous friend. From what I could sense as the circumstances of my arrival, he could well have judged it to be an impertinent imposition. Yet when we at once bought a house, and were faced with the task of moving into it the contents of several large crates brought from Adelaide, Professor Baxter and his wife turned up on us in boiler suits at eight o'clock in the morning, and fell to on the job. With the Baxters we were to exchange regular visits up to the time of their death, the one very soon after the other, some 20 years later.

Nevertheless, during my two years at Queen's I had to be a little careful with Baxter so far as his English Department was concerned. This was the easier in that there was, I believe, nowhere any very lively expectation that I could change the situation appreciably. Nobody with knowledge of how faculties are run in the provincial universities of Great Britain could have supposed such a thing. And Baxter was a man very attached and loyal to a *status quo*. There was also in his Department a certain mysterious Reader in English Language (or something of the sort) who lived 20 miles away and turned up at Queen's so seldom that during my two years there we happened never to meet. Baxter would clearly have been loath to approve any behaviour in strong contrast to this, and he early suggested to me that my teaching duties could readily be performed by my appearing on a couple of afternoons in the week. This was true. I seem to recall lecturing to two surprisingly small classes of pass students, and having dealings with two individuals — a young man and a young woman — who were reading for honours. This latter fact seems so odd that I am inclined to wonder whether my memory is betraying me. But I think it isn't so. During my time in Belfast there were just those two individuals in that category. And the one was a Catholic and the other a Protestant.

So here I come to the only point of much general interest about my impressions of Belfast in the later 1940s. Whether those two young people were in any sense close friends, I don't know. But they did, apparently, get along perfectly well together. And it seemed to be so with Protestants and Catholics at large. I was conscious, indeed, that tensions existed. There were more Protestants than Catholics — although the birth rates suggested it wouldn't always be the case. The Protestants were much more prosperous than the Catholics, and commanded the best jobs. Of this the Catholics were naturally resentful, and testified to the fact by here and there chalking up on walls the injunction, 'Kick the Pope'. As robust demotic utterance goes, the exhortation seemed surprisingly mild. Once, I recall, I went to some sort of quasi-Anglican church, and was startled to hear a sermon consisting of a diatribe against the Church of Rome. But throughout the community as a whole, although a certain unease may have been diffused, there was no detectable sense of impending calamity. And at least among the sort of people I chiefly met, the dichotomy chiefly felt was not one within Ulster itself, but rather one between North and South. Writers in particular seemed very conscious of being unable to hold up a candle to their fellows across the border: a reasonable modesty with O'Casey still living and Yeats and Joyce not long dead. The cultural heritage of Northern Ireland, in fact, seemed a meagre affair indeed when compared with that of Eire. 'Is Liffey worth leaving?' Joyce had asked. One answer seemed to be, 'Certainly not for anywhere beyond the Boyne.'

We were ourselves very contented. For the first time in our married life we owned the house we lived in. It had a pleasant garden, bounded on one side by the cabin of a conversable level-crossing keeper, and on the other by the mansion of the top man at Harland and Wolff, the shipbuilding concern which was the linchpin of Belfast's industrial prosperity. A short walk brought us into County Down: terrain at once familiar-seeming and beautiful. So we appeared to be done with *Sehnsucht* — which did, however, once attack us in an unexpected fashion. We were told that, in County Antrim and at no great distance from Belfast itself, there was an avenue of eucalypts. We went to look for them. And there, unbelievably, they were: the gum-trees of Australia once more — tettered, awkwardly angled, faintly ghostly even at noon. The sudden sight was formidable, but the scent was overwhelming. Momentarily, it was almost as if we were twelve thousand miles away from home.

If I was at all restless during the first of those two years, it was because of wondering whether, academically, Queen's marked the end of a road. Was I now to be rather like Wilfred Childe at the

University of Leeds: in employment providing a little useful routine, but with a mind slanted elsewhere? I wasn't very satisfied with this picture. Had I already embarked on the writing of 'straight' novels, it might have been different. But that was still some way ahead. And the Michael Innes stories (although I enjoyed writing them, or they wouldn't have such modest virtues as they do command) seldom occupied more than six weeks in the year. So there was distinctly something missing. Just what was missing, I doubt whether I more than vaguely knew. But David Wilson — ever my tutelary spirit — did: it was the discipline of a structured study of some period, or kind, of English literature. From Wilson, then, there came a letter. I opened it, read it, and (I clearly recall) turned to my wife wide-eyed. 'It seems I'm to be on the active list, after all,' I said.

I had been invited to write the final volume of *The Oxford History of English Literature*. I was a third choice, Wilson punctiliously explained. Edmund Wilson had been asked, and had replied — not altogether courteously — that he wasn't minded to read John Galsworthy again. V. S. Pritchett had been asked; had duly weighed the proposal; and had decided that he had better get on with novels and short stories. So now it was up to me: 'a practised writer', Wilson cautiously said.

Faced with this transformed situation (for it was that), I had at once, I believe, a fair notion of what I could, and what I couldn't, do. The volume had been given the provisional title of *Modern Literature*, which apparently meant picking up from about the time of Walter Pater and coming right up to date. For me, that was nonsense. It would be like holding a vast reception, with a nod and a handshake at the door to everybody who turned up. Only a library cormorant (to vary the figure and borrow from Coleridge) could contemplate such a thing. What I could do was spend the inside of a year with a major author, and then write 35,000 words on him. I was recklessly confident about that. And Wilson and his fellow general-editor, Bonamy Dobrée (who was another old friend) accepted it at once. My book was to be called *Eight Modern Writers*. All of them would have been alive in my own lifetime. And all of them would now be dead.

Such was my introduction to *OHEL* — which, uttered as an expletive, was what everybody concerned in the venture found comfortably expressive from time to time. The series was rather to lumber along. *Eight Modern Writers* certainly did. I seem to remember that the Delegates of the Clarendon Press intimated to me that they would expect my manuscript within two years, but as reasonable men might be disposed to allow me a third year if I judged it necessary. In fact, I took ten. (The Oxford *Ben Jonson*, after all, had taken Percy Simpson fifty.) And some of the projected volumes, I believe, haven't been published yet.

I would have been guileless indeed had I been unaware that my recruitment to *OHEL* portended a change of scene. We had arrived in Belfast early in January 1946, and we left for Oxford on the 23rd of June 1948. I was to become a Student of Christ Church, which (although for long *emeritus*) is what I am today.

Michael Innes (2) Detour into Thrillers

MICHAEL INNES HAD continued on the market with detective stories which (like Matthew Arnold in Max Beerbohm's cartoon) were not always wholly serious — being fairly regularly tinged, that is to say, with fantasy and extravagance. But another, and distinct, strain, emerged in some of them. It goes back not to Conan Doyle and G. K. Chesterton, but — I suppose — to two countrymen of my own, Robert Louis Stevenson and John Buchan. I have been told that *Lament for a Maker* smells strongly of *The Master of Ballantrae*, and although my memory of that story (read in 1924) doesn't quite respond to this, I am in no doubt about the validity of the general proposition. And that the detective element has to be rather awkwardly edged into *Lament for a Maker* is evident from the fact that my indefatigable official sleuth, John Appleby, arrives at Castle Erchany, the scene of action, only in the last third of the book. The mystery he investigates is not particularly memorable, but I regard this novel as leaving something in the mind, all the same — which is a quality not owned by the numerous Innes stories at all often.

The next book of any note is, I think, *The Secret Vanguard*, published in 1940 and set in the months immediately before the outbreak of the Second World War. It is essentially a spy thriller — and again Appleby, yet more awkwardly, undertakes the job of making it a detective story as well. There are, of course, many sorts of spy thrillers, and this one belongs to the sub-species that concerns a hunted man. Only my hunted man is a girl, and she is being hunted because she has, all-unawares, become involved in a totally preposterous espionage situation which no professional fabricator of spy stories would now look at for a moment. Secret agents pass information in railway carriages by spouting Swinburne to one another with bogus stanzas thrown in: absurdities like that. Yet the actual hunting of the girl, Sheila Grant, over a Scottish moor, is a different thing: far and away, I judge, the most empathic writing I have anywhere achieved. The chapters entitled 'Hawk' and 'Hare' are to my mind as good as such unassuming things can be. But again they have their derivations. Thus there comes a point at which Sheila is suddenly confronted by 'a curve of steel':

> For the first time she realized fully the significance of a railway line over such country as this. Unlike the undulating and heather-covered moor, it was something which, granted any sort of visibility at all, it would be virtually impossible to cross unobserved. And where a straight line might give scope for manoeuvre, this half-circle of track was like a pair of open jaws.

I believe the situation here comes straight from Buchan's *Prester John*. But almost immediately there follow the chapters called 'Sheila Travels without a Ticket', *'Johnny Cope'*, and 'Two in a Cage'. Here — and particularly in the appearance of Harry McQueen, the blind fiddler who peddles his 'poems of a Moray loon' up and down the line, and who can find his way through the glens by listening to the echoes from his instrument — I am drawing upon memories of my childhood. Harry's 'cage' is the stronghold, he believes, of that Alexander Stewart, the 'Wolf of Badenoch', who had burned down Elgin Cathedral at the close of the fourteenth century. The juxtaposition of Harry's crazy imaginings and the closely worked minute-by-minute account of Sheila's flight has the felicitousness that does sometimes drop unbidden into a writer's grasp. Here — to vary the figure — it lands me on a perch from which I descend clumsily enough. The closing chapters of *The Secret Vanguard* are a huddle of spy-and-detective stuff much lacking in clarity and credibility.

The Journeying Boy is a longer and more ambitious story than *The Secret Vanguard*, but with the same entirely conventional basic situation. An eminent scientist has made some discovery, vital to the defence of the realm, of which evilly disposed persons are plotting to gain possession. But whereas in the first book this scientist remains as thin as the scrap of paper on which his discovery can apparently be jotted down, in the second there is a determined attempt to make him three-dimensional. This is not, I think, wholly unsuccessful. Sir Bernard Paxton has adequate reality as a great scientist, and the suggestion of his being just that is enhanced by his consenting to live — unquestioningly and as if scarcely aware of the fact — as the man of substantial inherited wealth that he happens to be. He is also the widowed father of Humphrey Paxton, the journeying boy of the title, an imaginative, passionate, and emotionally volatile — or even nervously unstable — young adolescent, about whom he is anxiously caring but also hopelessly at sea. Nor is Sir Bernard, perhaps, a very good judge of grown men. It is luck (or, rather, a brisk subsidiary crime) that despatches Humphrey to the trap awaiting him in Ireland with a tutor as capable in tough situations as Mr Richard Thewless proves himself to be.

I find that in the first printing of the novel, Humphrey and Mr Thewless set out on their journey from London to Humphrey's unknown relations in Ireland on p. 33, and arrive there, severally and after a variety of mishaps, some 120 pages later. The first stage of this journey, that on the train from Euston to the port of Heysham, although set to this stately tempo, is crammed with alarms and suspicions and surprises. Thus Mr Thewless, roaming the train in a desperate search for a vanished Humphrey, comes upon 'an inert figure entirely swathed in bandages', guarded by 'an enormous Negro smoking a cigar'. He is, in fact, in the presence of 'Mr Wambus, professionally known as the Great Elasto, the India-rubber Man', and Mr Wambus is only one in a nightmarish collection of freaks, since the train is carrying a troupe of them. The train journey is thus across farcical territory in which nobody is what he seems to be, and the reader (it is no doubt hoped) is prepared for the same essential situation at the level not of comedy but of melodrama.

Belfast, 'grimly utilitarian and shrouded in rain', is unsympathetically treated — somewhat gracelessly, since I must have begun the book when living there happily enough. It has a railway station with 'a classical portico nicely painted to look like milk chocolate', and is liberally placarded with minatory texts based on scripture:

THEIR WORM DIETH NOT
AND THEIR FIRE IS NOT QUENCHED

Quickly, however, we are making another railway journey — on a narrow-gauge line which wanders into Eire. Here, although skulduggery eventually turns up in a tunnel, there are no designs upon the reader. On this Alice-in-Wonderland train I had myself lately travelled with a light-hearted enjoyment which I am simply trying to pass on. It leads, however, to the main scene of the novel's action: a run-down Irish country-house at an imaginary place called Killyboffin, and to an Atlantic seaboard of gigantic cliffs honeycombed with caves and caverns carrying subterranean waters far inland. I had seen just such cliffs at Malin Beg Head in the west of Donegal Bay. We are in Donegal — and it is a Donegal as real as I can make it. Whether at this point I am much excited by the larger contours of my story, I don't know. But the caves, and Humphrey's peril as he enters them with his treacherous kinsman, excite me very much, so that I have hard work to keep some sort of bridle on my prose. So we come to this:

> The rock face was damp and chill as they brushed it; and neither chill nor damp would wax or wane, whatever change befell external nature — for here the varying cycle of the year had no power to probe. Owning thus no pulse, no rhythm, the place was lifeless and ungenial, propagating only an unnatural and abundant brood of sounds. The waters that were now, as they climbed to a greater height, almost invisible beneath them, whispered ceaselessly like conspiring maniacs in some Tartarean bedlam. Single drops of water, falling from the fretted vault, exploded on polished stone with a strange resonance, like that of a distant harp-string snapping in an empty house at night. And their very footsteps, as if each in alarm at the other's tread, fled before them and behind them in a constantly repeated diminuendo of frenzied escape. When they spoke their voices, like every other sound, were distorted strangely, so that it was as if they were beset by their own travestied images in some hall of misshapen mirrors. And above them, as perceptibly present as if some muscular effort of their own must hold it off, was the vast suspended burden of living rock, so that one could think up through it until at length, at what might be almost an aeroplane's elevation, one came upon sheep nibbling the turf directly overhead.

It is after sundry episodes of adventure within this tremendous setting — episodes in which the kittle Humphrey shows himself resourceful and courageous in the highest degree — that the resolution comes with what is at least commendable speed. There have, it turns out, been two distinct gangs concerned to seize the boy as a means of coercing his eminent father into handing over his all-important papers. But now their game is up. The Eire *garda*, the Eire military have arrived at Killyboffin, as has a policeman from London in an aeroplane. So both sets of villains have to be got rid of. And here an idiosyncrasy of my own comes into play. I have always been reluctant to despatch my crooks and murderers to gaol or to the gallows, with the result that a high proportion of them meet with some form of poetic justice, are more or less ingeniously hoist with their own petard. So it is here. One lot have a speed-boat to escape in; the other lot find the London policeman's aeroplane unattended, and make off in it. But this second lot — our two prime villains during the latter part of the story —being without any experience of piloting a plane, crash within a couple of minutes of their taking the air. And they crash, of course, on the speed-boat, and thus the board is cleared at once. Mr Thewless sums up with the remark that Humphrey Paxton is a thoroughly capable boy, thus enunciating what is his highest commendation of a pupil.

It might be concluded from this résumé that *The Journeying Boy* is a simple adventure story, without any detective element. But this isn't quite so. Early in the action a certain Captain Cox has been found shot dead in a London cinema, for reasons which explain themselves much later in the novel. There are only the most slender clues to his identity and circumstances, and on these clues a Detective-Inspector of the Metropolitan Police called Cadover gets to work, his trail leading him finally to Killyboffin. Throughout the progress of the story there are flashes back to his activities in London, so that the sobriety of his investigation is set in contrast with the extravagant goings-on in Donegal. It is my impression that Cadover is rather a good police detective, and easier to believe in, often enough, than is John Appleby.

The Man from the Sea, published in 1955 and the last of this little group, is a straight thriller. There are plenty of inexplicabilities, but these resolve themselves in action and not through detective investigation. Apart from a village constable who remains off stage, there isn't a policeman in the book. Instead, there is something very like the hovering presence of Joseph Conrad. The young man upon whom the story opens, as he lies naked upon a Scottish beach at night in furtherance of a freakish amour with an older and married woman, is prone to brooding darkly on the difference between disgrace and dishonour — this as 'intermittently the sea, as if tired of vain whispering in the ear of night, heaved itself into a larger wave which splashed on the pale beach like the smack of a drowsily amorous hand'. And out of the sea comes another naked man. He is (I am sorry to say) a great scientist; his name is John Day; having defected to Russia some years before, and having recently (he declares) suffered an accident with some nuclear substance which must result in imminent death, he has contrived this spectacular return in order to make his peace with a deserted wife in London. At the end of the book we learn without much surprise that this is a spurious story. In Russia, Day has not been permitted to get right to the top; to do so is his consuming passion; he has therefore arranged to be picked up and shipped out of England by the representatives of some South American country in which he will be given the prime position he seeks.

As in *The Secret Vanguard*, the alien enemy in our midst proves capable of mobilizing improbably extensive forces with distinctly improbable speed. Moreover, for much of the book they are concerned to hunt down not a single person, as with Sheila Grant, but three people: Day; the young man of our first acquaintance in the story; and a girl cousin of the young man's who bobs up rather opportunely from Australia. It seems to me that to some extent they get in one another's way, complicating the topography of the chase to its disadvantage, since more concentration is required on the reader's part than is appropriate in the kind of entertainment on offer. What I recall with some satisfaction in the novel are certain vignettes of Scottish life and character: that and a fairly authentic command of demotic Scotch in the simpler characters. Sandy Morrison, resolute for adventure even if it puts in hazard his promotion from driving the ambulance to driving the hearse ('reverent-like') is my favourite here.

Michael Innes (3) Radio

IN CHRIST CHURCH there used occasionally to dine with us as a guest a man whom I came to think of as the real-life Higgins — the fictional Higgins being the phonological professor in Bernard Shaw's *Pygmalion*. This real-life Higgins was a professional person of some distinction, with no interest in any sort of phonetic science, but possessed of a fine ear which it had amused him to cultivate. He had only to listen to a few sentences uttered by anyone present to pick up, from within the received standard English common in the place, small indications of the precise corner of the globe the speaker came from. There was only one recorded occasion on which he appeared to have gone wrong, pronouncing the words 'West Riding' after listening to a man whose roots were deep in the south of England. But this man turned out to have been a prisoner of war for several years in circumstances which meant his hearing nothing except Yorkshire voices around him. With me the real-life Higgins had no difficulty at all. He said, 'Edinburgh, Edinburgh Academy', at once. This was the more satisfactory in that he might, I suppose, have said, 'Australia in childhood', or something of the sort. I had, in fact, found Australian speech the only positively and absolutely ugly thing in that extraordinary continent, and I had there probably preserved with care — and, perhaps, obtruded — the kind of modified southern English speech I had picked up partly at school but chiefly at Oxford.

A pommy accent was, of course, correspondingly ungrateful to many Australians, which may be one reason why I was very seldom asked to do any broadcasting in Adelaide. Nor did I much care for the activity. Those were primitive times, radio-wise. A man behind a sheet of glass would make commanding gestures enjoining either speeding up or slowing down — matters on which one would rather have trusted to one's own judgement. But quite early in my brief Belfast period I made a broadcast the substance of which I have totally forgotten, but which bore the distinctly cosy title, 'On Losing Oneself in a Book'. It was presently re-broadcast on what was then called the Third Programme, for which I was to do a good deal of writing in the years ahead. This quite unexpected activity, from which I was to gain a great deal of stimulus and enjoyment, came about entirely as a result of the renewal of an old Leeds association.

Rayner Heppenstall, who had been for a short time my pupil in the early 1930s, I can best describe as a kind of provincial Norman Cameron: extremely intelligent, essentially a poet, and totally uninterested in the academic study of literature for the purpose of acquiring a good university degree. Unlike Norman, and several young men of the same way of thinking with whom I was to become familiar at Christ Church, Rayner came from a simple background, and had gained a place at Leeds University only under some vicious system whereby he had pledged himself to employment as a schoolteacher for a certain term of years following graduation. What he actually did, I don't know. When the war came, and perhaps because in appearance he was far from robust (although in fact as tough as they come), he was clapped into the pay corps — the fact being declared by some coloured tabs or patches on his uniform, which he regarded as demeaning beyond the limits of speech. But in *The Blaze of Noon* he had already published a brilliant novel, and shortly after demobiliz-ation he found himself, along with the slightly older Louis MacNeice and one or two others, running for the BBC the Third Programme's 'Features' department. Just as Norman would have done about his job in advertising, Rayner affected impatient contempt for this employment, which he regularly referred to as 'the plumbing'. Nevertheless, he was an extremely talented producer, with a particular happiness in finding the right actor for a rôle, and an unexpected flair for coaxing actors of marked seniority and distinction to gather round his microphone and deliver themselves of their part.

My first piece for Rayner, called *Strange Intelligence*, is an imaginary conversation on an actual occasion: the visit paid by James Boswell and Dr Johnson to Lord Monboddo on Saturday, 21 August 1773. Boswell in his *Journal of a Tour to the Hebrides* puts himself on record as apprehensive about the meeting, since Johnson and Monboddo were known not to care for one another, and Johnson seemed unlikely now to converse amicably with one who believed man to have gradually elevated himself from an animal condition. Boswell, in fact, feared what he calls 'a violent altercation'. Nothing of the kind occurred — nor, of course, did I steer in any such direction my decorous neo-Landorian effort. The exchanges are in places astringent, but the adversaries remain civil. The total effect is rather stiff, and might well have been of pointless pastiche but for a remarkable performance by John Laurie as Monboddo. Laurie was to become most widely known a good many years later as a member of Dad's Army in the immensely popular television series with that title. But he was a remarkable actor in any Scottish rôle — and particularly so in Third Programme affairs, in which a quick grasp of current speculative interests was frequently required. Watching him in rehearsal working at bringing my first small theatre piece alive, I resolved to do him something more substantial if I possibly could. The result was *The Hawk and the Handsaw*, produced by Rayner some eighteen months later. *Strange Intelligence*, meanwhile, was published in a small volume containing roughly similar imaginary conversations by C. V. Wedgwood, Herbert Read, Rose Macaulay, Seán O'Faolain, V. S. Pritchett, and G. W. Stonier. But this keeping of literary company was only on a printed page. It was into the academic society of Oxford that I was at this time cautiously feeling my way.

Not that, at what may conceivably be called the intellectual level, my two worlds didn't connect. *Character and Motive in Shakespeare*, essentially an academic book, takes much of its colour from that sort of amateur interest in Freudian psychology which was fashionable in my generation. It attempts to show that what a powerful group of 'historical' critics were tending to write off as primitive, stagey and implausible in Shakespeare's characterization can in fact be vindicated or validated through a study of motives and mechanisms of behaviour uncovered by the new depth psychologies. For instance — I argued — nobody who has read Freud on the aetiology of delusional jealousy is likely to see as essentially theatrical, rubbishing, and 'unpsychological' the basic situation in *The Winter's Tale*. From the same area of interest came Michael Innes's *The Hawk and the Handsaw*. I had been much struck by Freud's brief comparison of *Hamlet* and the *Oedipus Tyrannus*, and impressed by the command of the huge field of *Hamlet* criticism exhibited by Freud's English disciple, Ernest Jones, in his expansion of Freud's seminal idea. Then an odd question came to me. *How would Hamlet have reacted had he been able to read Jones's notion of him?* I don't think I paused to consider just what I meant by '*Hamlet*' in this muzzy question. I simply sat down and began writing *The Hawk and the Handsaw*. The splendid part for John Laurie had come to me. He would *be* Freud-cum-Jones. He would also have been Lady Macbeth's Scottish physician who, away and clear from Dunsinane, has found fresh court employment at Elsinore. There, on the battlements, he would explain to Hamlet Hamlet's mystery. With what result, I didn't know. That would appear.

The Hawk and the Handsaw is elaborately, and I think not unskilfully, structured. Practice in the fabricating of detective-story plots must have helped me here, but the transitions in both time and place might well have remained confusing save for Rayner's consummate producing of the piece. One tends to think of 'sound effects' as a rather trifling element in dramatic illusion; Rayner had mastered the craft of so employing them that they simultaneously created *ambiance* and clarified action. And the action here is intricate enough. It opens upon an Elsinore in which the death of young Prince Hamlet lies some 40 years back. Fortinbras has for long been King of Denmark; Horatio (who has developed a hint of Polonius-like foxiness) is his Lord Chamberlain; tucked away in a wind-scoured turret is an old and discredited court physician, Dr Mungo: he and his serving boy read to one another from an English book, Timothy Bright's *A Treatise of Melancholie*. A troupe of strolling players has arrived at Elsinore, with Shakespeare's *Hamlet* in their repertory; and this play Horatio causes to be acted before the court, seeing that it may be made the occasion of a demonstration of loyalty to Fortinbras. Snatches of the dialogue float up to Mungo and his servant as the wind again and again blows open the door at the head of their winding stair. Several tricky transitions have to follow, since Mungo has to be brought into colloquy with King Fortinbras, and within this colloquy have to be set, as direct encounter fully dramatized on the battlements of the castle, the two psychiatric sessions (as they may be termed) between the young prince and the doctor fresh from Dunsinane: these constituting the core of *The Hawk and the Handsaw*. Hamlet rejects with some eloquence the Oedipal explanation of his conduct, but then reflects that 'here is no issue to pass on at the jump', and promises that, on his way to England, he will 'think precisely on this night's event'. Fortinbras, finally addressing Dr Mungo, ventures a little deeper:

> For Hamlet, who had such reach of mind, were those doubts you sowed not somewhat larger than any concerning the mere matter — grave though that was — of old King Hamlet's end? Had you not opened to him, perhaps, the vision of a climate too chill for the tree of the knowledge of good and evil to grow and bear in? And did his last dejection come from this: that you had shown him reason as having no reach beyond the moon, but as a dweller wholly amid things corruptible?

Mungo's immediate conclusion is naturally that Fortinbras stands much in need of analysis himself, and he puts a hopeful question: 'May I ask if your majesty is with any frequency graciously pleased to dream?' And so we reach an end:

> FORTINBRAS (hastily): No, no, good Doctor, my dreams shall be my own, and any ghosts that haunt me private to myself. We thank you and excuse you. Now, good night.
>
> DOCTOR: I am your majesty's devoted subject and — may I remind you? — most careful physician upon any issue.
>
> *The tap of the* DOCTOR's *stick is heard as he withdraws from the royal presence; its tempo changes as he begins to climb the winding stair, and at the same time he falls to muttering.*
>
> DOCTOR: Barbarians . . . freebooters and pirates . . . that I should have to end my days in the most comfortless corner of a brigand's den!
>
> BOY: Nay, master, be more cheerful. Did not the king — although he may have understood you not — speak of a purse? I judge that you shall have some profit of this night's work.
>
> DOCTOR (with a snarl): Profit? Profit! I tell you, boy, were I from Elsinore away and clear, *profit* again should hardly draw me here!
>
> *The sound of the wind and the waves has been growing as they climb, and the deep reverberation of the breakers is heard at the Close.*

The production of *The Hawk and the Handsaw* had an odd sequel. Returning from London to Oxford on a late train (familiarly known, I believe, as the Fornicator) after the first broadcast, I was assailed by a sudden anxiety. Surely I had pillaged from Ernest Jones's work wholesale, and had then, in Dr Mungo, cast ridicule on its author? Did the outraged Jones's mind move in the direction of libel, neither the BBC nor I would have a leg to stand on! This absurd panic lingered in my mind, if intermittently and obscurely, for some days. Then one morning, sure enough, there was a letter on my breakfast-table addressed in what I saw at once was a neat medical hand. And it indeed proved to be from Ernest Jones. What it said, however, was that he had unfortunately missed the earlier part of my play, and would be grateful if I could send him a copy of it. This I did, and received in return an off-print of a paper by Jones, 'The Death of Hamlet's Father', from the *International Journal of Psycho-Analysis*. After this, we corresponded from time to time. Jones pointed out a shade reproachfully that I had neglected in *Hamlet* the homosexual significance of the method adopted by Claudius in murdering King Hamlet in his orchard.

Perhaps because of this quite tenuous association — and perhaps, too, because under my own name I had somewhere reviewed all three volumes of Jones's *Life of Freud* — I was invited some years later by what was called, I think, the British Psycho-Analytical Society to deliver the triennial Ernest Jones Memorial Lecture. Rashly, perhaps, I accepted the invitation, and the lecture duly took place in London before a large gathering which must have consisted, in the main, of the assembled psycho-analysts of Great Britain. What was expected of me, I suppose, was some extension to literature in general of such findings of analytical psychology as can be handled by a lay literary critic. This being beyond me, I tried to discuss the problems that attend writing for the common reader the biography of a savant whose achievement has been in some predominantly abstruse field of knowledge. I can recall being determined to get through my lecture without perpetrating what my auditory would have called a *parapraxis*. This, no doubt, was levity. I was making quite a serious effort, all the same.

After the lecture there was a reception. It took place in a large and rather bleak hall, the only adornment of which was a very big photograph of Freud. In the course of this entertainment somebody introduced to me as holding secretarial office relieved me of my script. This was much in the common way of such formal affairs, in which the lecturer has delivered himself from a full text, such as may subsequently be reproduced in a journal. So I handed over my Ernest Jones Memorial Lecture — which, contrary to my normal practice, happened to exist only in this single copy. I never saw it again. But several years later a member of the Society who had been present on the occasion thought to make some inquiry about it—of course at no prompting from me. But his curiosity was unsatisfied. So, too, is mine. Did my offering somewhere go badly wrong? I shall never know.

From one small mystery to another: *The Mysterious Affair at Elsinore.* I wrote this short piece, and myself delivered it on the Third Programme, at about the time *The Hawk and the Handsaw* was incubating. It is a joke in which I show—with all the ingenuity Michael Innes can command — that everything happening in *Hamlet* proceeds from Fortinbras's ruthlessly clearing his way to the throne of Denmark. Does he not say *Take up the bodies* when every policeman knows that in a situation involving homicide the bodies must on no account be moved? When Claudius declares that he is *but hurt* does not Fortinbras instantly command that *the soldiers' music and the rite of war speak loudly*, thus drowning anything the dying king may say beneath the blended uproars of a peal of ordnance and a military band?

The success of this sort of thing (of which Maurice Morgann's 'Essay on the Dramatic Character of Sir John Falstaff' is the archetype) consists in the apparent thoroughness with which every aspect of a case appears to have been considered; and this canon may have led me into rather more elaboration than the joke deserved. But in subsequent years its length proved just right for reading to any of the undergraduate literary societies in which Oxford colleges then abounded. Once, rather late in its career, I took it to Balliol, being by that time convinced that it at least squeezed the last drop of absurdity from the orange of Shakespeare's play. I was listened to by the young men with attention. They then proceeded to turn my piece upside down and inside out with a degree of fantastic invention before which my own uneffectual fire decidedly paled. I was constrained to believe (as Balliol men tend to believe) that Balliol men are very clever indeed.

Almost to the end of the 1950s I continued to supply Rayner with small dramatic pieces for the Third Programme. Into one of them, called *A Visit to Bly*, I was seduced by the thought that, driving to the scene of *The Turn of the Screw* in Edith Wharton's car, Henry James could be exhibited as suddenly alarmed by a roadside notice familiar to my childhood, which had read:

MOTORISTS! BEWARE OF THE CHILDREN.

Apart from this, I stuck to Shakespeare and Shakespeare criticism: simply, no doubt, because they remained the subjects in which I was reasonably well-seen. None of these later broadcasts has ever been published. I print one of them now.

Michael Innes (4) Mr W. H.

WHEN THOMAS THORPE published Shakespeare's Sonnets in 1609 he wished to their 'onlie begetter . . . Mr W. H. all happinesse and that eternitie promised by our ever-living poet'. This piece is based on the common assumption that Mr W. H. is the 'lovely boy' to whom the majority of the sonnets appear to be addressed, and on the conjecture that the 77th sonnet comments upon certain presents he received on his fourteenth or fifteenth birthday. The scene is Venice, and the date a little before 1640.

POET'S VOICE. Oh thou, my lovely boy, who in thy power
     Dost hold Time's fickle glass his fickle hour;
     Who hast by waning grown, and therein show'st
     Thy lover's withering as thy sweet self grow'st;
     If nature, sovereign mistress over wrack,
     As thou go'st onwards, still will pluck thee back,
     She keeps thee to this purpose, that her skill
     May time disgrace and wretched minutes kill.
     Yet fear her, O thou minion of her pleasure!
     She may detain, but not still keep, her treasure:
      Her audit, though delay'd, answer'd must be,
      And her quietus is to render thee.

The music of Monteverdi, and Venetian 'sound effects', punctuate the piece, here and later.

TUTOR. . . . and on the following day, the twentieth of June, the wind being fair, arrived at that most queenly city. The pilot boat having met with us, and our certificate of *contamacia* being presently allowed by *gli seniori de la Sanità*, we passed by two castles until we came to St Mark's place, and thence by *gondola* (as they call their light craft) to *Canalgrande* and under *Rialto* bridge, curiously compacted together with only one arch, and the fairest by many degrees that ever I saw, read, or heard of.

138

The gondola is heard, moving through the water.

LORD. What news on the Rialto?

TUTOR. My lord?

LORD. Do not you remember, good Master Neville, the old play of the Venetian Jew? I wonder, now: where would Belmont be?

TUTOR. Our lodging is to be by the Cannaregio; and it is vouched for as a well-reputed quarter, heaven be praised. . . . Belmont, my lord?

LORD.   In Belmont is a lady richly left,
        And she is fair, and, fairer than that word,
        Of wondrous virtues. Sometimes from her eyes ——

TUTOR. Of many Venetian ladies, my lord, the virtue is not, by all accounts, so wondrous. And we are come here for other studies.

LORD. [*laughing*] Nor is the wide world ignorant of her worth,
        For the four winds blow in from every coast
        Renowned suitors, and her sunny locks
        Hang on her temples like a golden fleece,
        Which makes her seat of Belmont Colchos'
        strand,
        And many Jasons come in quest of her.
  Oh, my Antonio — oh, my good Master Neville, I should say — think you *I* might bear away a Portia from this Venice?

TUTOR. And what would the noble earl, your father, have to say to your tutor then, my lord? Nothing but hail and farewell, I trow. Yes, indeed; I should have my quietus quickly. Let not that honey-tongued Shakespeare's fond imaginations represent this same Venice to thee as a place for vain and amatorious thoughts. Tomorrow must we to the Arsenal with our letters, that thou mayst make those martial observations which thy father hath appointed thee.

LORD. Right willingly. They say it is an eighth wonder of the world. It would be there that the Moor did equip himself before making sail for the defence of Cyprus.

TUTOR. The Moor? Nay, I have you. And there is in *Othello*, indeed, matter of some gravity, well expressed in poesy rising to the height of Sophocles his style.

LORD.   The tyrant custom, most grave senators,
        Hath made the flinty and steel couch of war

My thrice-driven bed of down: I do agnize
A natural and prompt alacrity
I find in hardness ——

TUTOR. Aye, it is well enough to stir the blood. But there is in it, too, what must please the wiser sort; and which is as yet — I thank heaven for it, boy — beyond the tether of thy comprehension. Betwixt the Merchant's Venice and the Moor's (though both be this same dream-like town, half marble and half water) there lie many leagues of disenchantment and pain. Perfidy, suspicion, jealousy, despair: such were the milestones on thy Shakespeare's progress, maybe. . . . But here is a strange discourse to be fallen upon even as these fellows prepare to tie up at what must be our quay. Mark how yonder boatmen, turning in and out of their narrow canals, leave but the thinness of a foil between their long craft and the very houses. And hark to the cries by which each gives warning of his movements to the others. These are sounds more musical than our London watermen reach to. And now one sings a water-music.

LORD. Belmont was your place for music!

The sound of the traffic of the canals has been reinforced by a distant barcarole. As the gondola comes to rest there is a sudden babble of Italian voices, raised in welcome and solicitation. All this then ceases abruptly.

TUTOR. Our lodging was at a very fair house, most handsomely furnished with hangings, beds, tables and the like, all exceeding rich, together with great abundance of curious chairs, linen and plate. The chimneypieces were of fine marble, being statues of gods and goddesses chaste in design but of too liberal a fancy, the like being true also of much most excellent carved work which did wonderfully adorn the rooms. This house, and thereto a small garden full of fine devices and images in marble or bronze, belonging to one of the *Clarissimi* of the place lately gone abroad upon state affairs, was by the kind offices of our ambassador (a right worthy friend of my lord's father) appointed us during our repair in Venice. And now it was wonderful to see how my young lord, a most dear and hopeful boy, who had during our Paduan sojourn most long and faithfully beaten his brains alike at Ciceronianism and the mathematicals, did, as if in the sunshine of this place, shoot, exfoliate and blossom into a luxurance of sense and fancy. At the Arsenal, indeed, he diligently noted sundry matters proper to one who must, under God's favour, come to great place: as of the casting of ordnance, the ordering of great rooms open at both ends for building new galleys, the manner of storing arms preparative to the sudden sending forth of armies, and other like matters of martial worth and dignity. Yet here I marked that nothing more largely took his fancy than a certain great toy or gee-gaw employed by the Duke and *Serenissimi* upon their high occasions: to wit a vessel like a galley, called *Bucentoro*, whereon is shewed the uttermost of art for carved work, that being over-layed with gold, when she is in the water, she appears to be all of pure gold. And as he made survey of this he read upon the same in a book brought with him out of England: those travels idly styled his *Crudities* by the late worthy Master Coryat.

Faintly, as from below, the sound of the Venetian crowd.

LORD. [*reading*] 'The fairest galley of all is the *Bucentoro*, the upper parts whereof in the outside are richly gilt. It is a thing of marvellous worth, the richest galley of all the world, so exceeding glorious that I never heard or read of the like in any place, these only excepted, *videlicet*: that of Cleopatra, which she so exceedingly sumptuously adorned with cables of silk and other passing beautiful ornaments; and those that the Emperor Caligula ——' But yes! Master Neville: do you remember?

> The barge she sat in, like a burnish'd throne,
> Burn'd on the water; the poop was beaten gold;
> Purple the sails ——

But how goes it on? There is something about silken cables. . . . But I cannot remember it.

TUTOR. The learned historiographer Plutarch largely describes the same. But I never heard your poetry. Is it from another of your old plays?

LORD. It is from the play of Antony and Cleopatra in the great folio of Shakespeare's works given me by my lady mother against my last birthday.

TUTOR. Boy, boy — thy head is too full by far of all that vain matter. A poet can surely find more godly work than to write of Cleopatra and her Antony, famous patterns of unlawful love as they are.

LORD. I have heard that his majesty King Charles himself reads often in Shakespeare's book, and hath indeed honoured it with annotations in his own hand.

TUTOR. His majesty is not, as thou art, sixteen years old, and a twig like to take any bent applied to it.

LORD. He *must* have been here!

TUTOR. The king, my lord? I never heard ——

LORD. Nay, not the king: Gog, Magog and old Father Thames preserve him! Shakespeare, Master Neville! For turn and look. Could a man write poetry — *his* poetry — *without* having seen this Venice, itself the only poem of Christendom? I never knew what eyes were, until I came here. But *they* have always known, who framed these towers and domes between sea and sky. Were ever such curious universal artists, whether in marble or bronze or painter's pigments? Day after day, as we have strolled in the great cool churches, or lingered in those palaces to whose owners we have paid our ceremonial duty, or stood in that square, beyond all admiring, rightly by old Coryat called rather *Orbis* than *Urbis Forum*; day after day I have felt grow on me the wish that it were here and not in my own barbarian country that my patrimony lay. To be a Magnifico of Venice, Neville, with poets to sing for me ——

TUTOR. Aretino, belike, my lord — who, crippled by a rival in some low amour, here spent his last years in profligate living, in penning licentious dialogues, and in flattering rich and foolish patrons.

LORD. —— and one such as that rare fellow Titian to decorate my cabinet! Were this not better than to lord it in grey Whitehall, amid mouldy hangings cobbled up by Flemish boors?

TUTOR. And what wouldst thou have Titian — or Titian's shade — paint for thee, my lord?

LORD. Venus! Venus rising from the sea; nay, rising from yonder lagoon at my very own water gate!

TUTOR. Dear lad, here, under this southern climature, all seems to me sensual and heartless. And that, maybe, is very well for the young. But thou too must grow old one day, as I myself, verily, a little begin to do. And how would thy Titians content thee when all thy limbs and members were shrunken and sapless beneath thy furred gown? This is no country for old men.

LORD. But it is for the young — [*low*] in one another's arms!

TUTOR. Alas! Titian, I see — if not Aretino — has gained a scholar in these last days. But meanwhile our studies halt. There is the making of the sails to inquire into.

LORD. They are made by women, Master Neville. Belike you should lead your young bear another way.

TUTOR. [*displeased*] This is very idle talk that we are fallen upon. I would not wish to check thy observations of all that is rare and excellent in kind in this place, as I grant thee are even Titian's trollops, sprawled in their necklaces and nakedness.

LORD. Perhaps it was not always as trollops that they pleased him, Master Neville. He was a hundred or thereabouts, men say, when he pained some.

TUTOR. Then God give thee, dear lad, better employment in thy own centenary of years! And I, for one, would not grow old in Venice. 'Tis a thing that only Venetians may with tolerable safety do. Here, indeed, comes all the world having money in its purse and an itch for liberty and naughtiness. And not the gross and simple lewdness of our Bankside, either; but curious luxury to tickle decaying palates, or help procrastinate an old lecher's impotent years. There can be small hope of salvation in such a close.

LORD. [*laughing, but with affection and gaiety*] Lord, Lord: if here be not a sermon for young citizens at Paul's Cross — or such as shall largely correct the lickerous Benchers of an Inn! But for me, Master Neville, it is without pertinency. I do not think that I shall grow old. I have not a mind to it. Rather I shall remain, as you say, sensual and heartless, with painters to paint me wildernesses of trollops, and musicians to compose me love-songs, and poets to rhyme of me as ever young and ever fair. For mortality is an unhandsome thing. [*The dull report of a cannon is heard as from a distance, and from an answering distance bells chime.*] Master Neville! What is that?

TUTOR. It is the signal of noon, my lord. Another of thy hours is fled.

The bells continue to chime for a few seconds before fading.

TUTOR. And now did it begin clearly to appear that my young lord was a bear (as he pleasantly called himself) not gratefully to be led on too short a chain; nor did I judge it prudent to inhibit his free coming and going about the monuments and curiosities of the place. And indeed so stored or (I may say) farced is that city with remarkable works both of antique times and of new that it is scarcely to be reckoned how much profit of learning (whether politic, civil, or philosophic) may be gathered of a mute conversation with its very stones. And as for the safety and good order of the common streets and waterways, these (bating one particular alone) are such that the nobles and gentlemen do everywhere pass freely and unattended, it being only of a night-time that certain desperate men called Braves are like to commit their horrid villainies, wandering abroad to stab and rifle such as they may make their prey. But the particular hazard of which I speak is this, that many of the boatmen (and especially such as attend for hire by *Rialto* bridge) are like to carry the unwary traveller not about his express and declared business, but rather to some one of those naughty and sumptuous houses, full (they say) of fair rooms most glorious and glittering to behold, where inhabit the famoused and notorious courtesans of Venice, the like of whom (as men rehearsed in this unholy study will declare to you) are nowhere else in all Christendom to be found.

The voice of the young lord is heard at a distance, delivering itself of 'Lasciatemi morire', and his footsteps approach in echoing acoustic.

TUTOR. [*muttering*] Here the lad comes, up that great marble staircase with its unseemly goddesses; and in his head, I fear, some new lightness or folly. What company does he keep these days?

LORD. [*breaking off his singing as he enters the room*] Nay, Master Neville, look not so censorious. This is music by a most holy and religious man, lately indeed become a priest, and for long *maestro di capella* (as they say) in the cathedral of this very town: one Claudio Monteverde. Lord, how hungry am I! Does our dinner wait? [*He sings again.*]

TUTOR. And who, my lord, has been teaching thee this most godly or priestly music?

LORD. An Englishman. [*He begins another stave, thinks better of it, and declaims instead:*] Venegia, Venegia, chi non te vede non te pregia!

TUTOR. An Englishman? Hath the worthy Ambassador — ?

LORD. [*who is collecting a decanter*] Nay, Neville: the Ambassador
hath no more ear than an adder, even as you have no more eye
than a newt. But this Englishman hath both eye and ear: yes,
and palate too. Or *had*. [*Thoughtfully*] Indeed, *had* were perhaps
better. [*He seats himself at table.*]

TUTOR. [*also sitting down*] Palate?

LORD. For wines, Master Neville. It appeareth that there is a
veritable science of them, into which a man may notably
research, and to a marvellous profit. Now, this Muscadine [*he
is pouring out a glass as he speaks*] of which we take our common
refection, is after all, it seems, but a common stuff. But your
Liatico is another matter. Your Liatico is a very cordial and
generous liquor. And your Romania, too, is not to be despised.
But the pearl of all (the very hippocrene, Master Neville) is
your Lachrima Christi. [*He begins to eat.*]

TUTOR. [*shocked*] Lachrima Christi . . . a wine so named? What
blasphemy is this! And in what else has the Englishman been
entering thee?

LORD. Women.

TUTOR. [*distressed, but resigned: for this is not his first bear*] I feared it.
My dear Lord, I hope that the bawdy-house was at least one
frequented only by persons of rank.

LORD. Bawdy-house? Neville, Neville, my dear tutor: how
lewd a mind hast thou. This was no bawdy-house. It was a
theatre, and the women most lovely, expert and noble actors
— or actresses, as it may be proper to call 'em.

TUTOR. [*this time very shocked*] Women acting in a theatre! An
abomination, my lord; a flat abomination.

LORD. And then he took me — my Englishman — to view the
Mountebanks or Charlatans: a sort of cross betwixt players and
peddlers, and (I declare) the oddest and most facete fellows in
the world. There was one, a dwarf, intent to sell some rubbish
of medicinal oils or sovereign waters, that made us an
extemporal speech ——

TUTOR. [*interrupting*] Is this countryman of ours (whose familiar
acquaintance you appear to have made, and all in a breath) a
person of quality, my lord?

LORD. [*checked*] Of quality? He is a private gentleman. A *poor*
private gentleman.

TUTOR. Then heaven pity him, boy, in this predatory place.
How poor?

LORD. [*who is eating cheerfully*] Not so poor as when I met him. He had a fistful of gazets of me ere we parted.

TUTOR. A gentleman, and took coppers from a stranger's bounty?

LORD. I did not think that pride would let him take more. This was only on the pretence that he had left his purse at his lodging, and so lacked a few pence to cast to a waterman. [*He stops eating, and adds soberly:*] He is, indeed, a broken gentleman, Master Neville. And, what is more, he is old.

TUTOR. In Venice there be such broken men of every nation, and it is commonly no good course of life that has brought them here. Thou sayst he is old? But I have heard thee call *me* old, child that thou art.

LORD. My Englishman will not see threescore again.

TUTOR. Then heaven pity him, indeed.

LORD. He seemed to ask no pity of men.

TUTOR. But only gazets?

LORD. Yes: a sort of beggar. But a gay one — when his pains racked him not. For he hath, I hear, some heavy disease: I cannot guess what. Perhaps too much Lachrima Christi doth afflict him.

TUTOR. Or maybe too much of something with a different name. He sounds not a wholesome companion, dear my lord. Nor one, surely that should much attract thee, despite his knowledge of playhouses and mountebanks and wines. Or has he more than that?

LORD. Beauty.

TUTOR. [*startled*] Beauty — a man broken, diseased, and of threescore years or more?

LORD. A kind of ruined beauty. [*He is silent, and then adds, as in sudden discovery:*] Even such, Master Neville, as I think this city, with all its treasures, doth begin to wear.

There crashes in a clangour of many bells, with which are presently mingled the voices of the Venetian populace, celebrating the Festa of the tenth of July. This develops behind the tutor's succeeding speech into a montage proper to his account: a professional march, an ecclesiastical chant, strains of Monteverde, and instrumental dance music are distinguishable amid the general noises of popular celebration.

TUTOR. And now I must tell you that on the tenth of July, being the anniversary of the miraculous staying by God's grace of a great pestilence that did aforetime afflict their city, the people of Venice make a holy day or *festa* with certain special and extraordinary solemnities, as the going of the Duke and Senators, all richly attired, in solemn procession to the church called of the Redeemer: a progress made across the very sea itself on a fair broad bridge consisting of boats very artificially joined together. But what is above all remarkable, nor ever too much to be wondered at by such as come from more sober and phlegmatical climes, is the great merriment and abundant cheer upon which this serious and religious day closes. For the people of every quality (nay, not bating the red damask-gowned *Clarissimi* and *Serenissimi* themselves) do mask and out upon the squares, streets and waters of the place, there with feasting and singing (yea, and even with divers kinds of gambols, frisk or morris: sometimes without and sometimes within the very churches) to pass the time in most gamesome, idle, and (as a man may say) phrenetical sort. Now my young lord and I being towards the close of evening on this same *festa* gone abroad to view the singularity thereof, and having but hardly passed through the press of people in that great square which, like the very presence-chamber of Christendom, standeth hard by the church of St Mark. . . .

The tutor's voice has faded behind the singing of the crowd, which grows for some moments in volume and then itself fades. But we continue to hear music as a dark instrumental undertow until the voices of the crowd erupt again.

LORD. This way, Neville: this way, I say! Give the hulking fellow your shoulder, and follow me. I hear high revel down yonder *calle*.

TUTOR. Low revel, I had rather call it, my lord. For here already are only the dwellings of mechanical people. Phaw — what a stinking lane is this, and yet yon church at but a stone's throw!

LORD. 'Tis but London again, as to that. And now over this bridge. I recall it from day-time. They name it the *ponte del paradiso*.

TUTOR. I like it not. It smells of a worse place. Paradise: God save the mark!

LORD. And now it opens upon a little tumble-down *piazza* — a *piazzetta* is the word. And here is revel uncouth enough: if it be not rather misery.

The background sounds have changed character. The singing is coarse, drunken, and fragmentary. Amid a variety of voices a man and woman can be heard quarrelling fiercely, and a second man delivers himself of a monologue suggestive of maudlin despair. Above this and the like clamour an old man's voice is presently heard.

OLD MAN. (*within*) Succour! For the love of Jesus . . . succour!

(*There is instant silence, which is held for some seconds.*)

TUTOR. And so, wandering those narrow streets for our diversion on that disordered night, by chance we came upon him: my young lord's old Englishman, the same that had, but two days' space before this, discoursed so sagely of your Liatico and Lachrima Christi. A pitcher of water was all his interest now. Poor man, he lay on straw in a wretched room, without so much as a taper's light until my lord's slender store of Italian, and his opened purse, gained him that small accommodation. It lit features ruined, indeed: but yet, as my lord had said, holding something of a past beauty. He was dying — and under some constant fretting care. Not — alas! — for his soul's salvation. His thought (when, indeed, it did not wander in plain delirium) was set vainly on his last remaining worldly possession: a pocket watch, no less, which he held still jealously guarded beneath his own fast putrefying flesh.

OLD MAN. The dial . . . the rascals would have the dial. Thieves . . . all thieves, boy, in this whoreson place. Would that I had never seen its Circean beauty! They have taken my sword: the sword of one of good family, mark you, boy. They have taken the signet-ring my grandsire gave me. And now, when I die, they will take the dial: the birthday dial I had of my father when I was about thy age, lad, or something less.

LORD. They shall not have your dial, good friend. Both I, and my tutor here, Master Neville, warrant it.

OLD MAN. *Thy* tutor? I cannot see . . . nor scarcely hear. Thou art a gentleman?

TUTOR. You speak to a young nobleman, sir: one travelling abroad with me for his better instruction.

OLD MAN. [*not so wandering that he fails to be impressed*] My duty to your lordship, and to you, worthy sir. I too (a gentleman of ancient lineage, an't please you) had a tutor once. A strange fantastical fellow that wrote verses.

LORD. [*quickly curious*] Verses?

OLD MAN. Water . . . water again. . . . Aye, verses, God save
the mark. As of this very dial my father gave me at the term of
my fourteenth year. And my mother gave me a glass. She was
vain of *her* looks as reflected in *my* looks, God rest her soul.
And my grandam gave me a holy volume, filled with most
pious and unreadable sentences.

LORD. And your tutor: did he give you aught?

OLD MAN. A commonplace book. [*Laughing*] A commonplace
book, wherein I might digest my reading: and on the fly-leaf a
copy of the worthy pedant's own verses. I think I can recall
them now. [*He recites, with a little uncertainty*:]

> Thy glass will show thee how thy beauties wear,
> Thy dial how thy precious minutes waste;
> These vacant leaves thy mind's imprint will bear,
> And of this book this learning mayst thou taste.
> The wrinkles which thy glass will truly show
> Of mouthed graves will give thee memory;
> Thou by thy dial's shady stealth mayst know
> Time's thievish progress to eternity ———

LORD. 'Time's thievish progress to eternity'!

OLD MAN. Aye, aye: verily such stuff as that. As for my
grandam's pious tome and my tutor's blank paper: I lost them
both quickly enough, I doubt not. And the looking-glass I
broke over my young brother's head for mocking me as I
gazed in it. But I have the dial still, and these pestilent knaves
shall not lay their hands on it. The dial will to the grave with
me . . . when, in the fulness of time, I am old, and that day
comes. [*He groans from pain or weakness, and resumes with sudden
apprehensiveness and a growing wildness.*] Old? Did you say old?
Tell yon horned and long-tailed fellow in the corner I am not
minded to it. . . . I am not minded to grow old, I say!

LORD. [*softly*] Not minded to grow old! Did this tutor write you
other verses?

OLD MAN. Aye, marry — and again of that same looking-glass,
when my mother was so fondly fain that I should be betrothed
to our good neighbour's plain daughter: myself still a boy,
forsooth, that had never seen or tasted the *bona-robas* of the
Bankside. 'Look in thy glass' [*he is painfully remembering*] —
'Look in thy glass, and tell the face thou viewest now is the
time that face should form another.' [*Laughs*] Aye, much

strange stuff of that feather. And threats, too, mark you: threats to make the young flesh creep. 'When forty winters shall besiege thy brow, and dig deep trenches in thy beauty's field.' Stuff, too, about being death's conquest, and making worms my heir. [*Whispers*] But I tell you, friends, I am not minded to grow old.

LORD. His wit wanders, Master Neville. Think you he might be moved to our lodgings?

TUTOR. If it be your wish, my lord, in the morning we may venture it. But, indeed, I think he will never from this place.

LORD. Strange matter this, of the rhyming tutor. Did *you* ever rhyme, Master Neville? And, did you so, I wonder were your verses good?

OLD MAN. When I do count the clock that tells the time,
            And see the brave day sunk in hideous night;
            When I behold the violet past prime,
            And sable curls all silver'd o'er with white . . .

The old man's voice has grown weaker as it recites this quatrain, the last line of which is heard synchronously as spoken by the poet's voice, which then continues alone:

POET'S VOICE. . . . When lofty trees I see barren of leaves,
              Which erst from heat did canopy the herd,
              And summer's green, all girded up in sheaves,
              Borne on the bier with white and bristly beard;
              Then of thy beauty do I question make,
              That thou among the wastes of Time must go —

The poet's voice has gone on echo, and fades behind a long, deep groan from the old man. A moment's silence succeeds, and then a bell is heard.

LORD. [*quietly*] Two of the clock.

TUTOR. The *festa* is over, praise be to God. Yet I think I still hear singing on the water. This Venice is a place full of voices.

LORD. [*startled*] Voices?

TUTOR. And music: always music. Hark!

Faintly in the distance a barcarole is heard. As it fades there comes a long sigh from the old man.

LORD. He stirs again. I would that the Ambassador's physician were come. Another of these talking fits (be it about his rhyming tutor or another) is like to finish him.

TUTOR. The doctor will have been revelling with the rest, and we must be patient. Nor, dear boy, do I think any physic can help this man.

LORD. [*softly*] 'When forty winters shall besiege thy brow.
　　　　　　'And dig deep trenches in thy beauty's field. . . .'
I could almost believe, Neville —— But no matter.

OLD MAN. [*in a clear voice*] Have you a poem for me this morning, Master Will?

POET'S VOICE. Devouring Time, blunt thou the lion's paws,
　　　　　And make the earth devour her own sweet brood;
　　　　　Pluck the keen teeth from the fierce tiger's jaws,
　　　　　And burn the long-liv'd phoenix in her blood;
　　　　　Make glad and sorry seasons as thou fleets,
　　　　　And do whate'er thou wilt, swift-footed Time,
　　　　　To the wide world and all her fading sweets;
　　　　　But I forbid thee one most heinous crime:
　　　　　O, carve not with thy hours my love's fair brow,
　　　　　Nor draw no lines there with thine antique pen —

The poet's voice has gone on echo, and faded.

OLD MAN. [*fretful, querulous*] I said, have you no poem for me this morning?

TUTOR. Alas, how should he have any answer? The tutor must be dead ere this, and he calls upon a voice that none will hear again. . . . You have slumbered, friend. Has sleep done you any ease?

OLD MAN. Sleep! And what if I did sleep with her — and that (as thou saidst) before my lip was rough and razorable? The better man I! What though she were thy mistress, good pedant, and thou hadst written me a world of sonnets? She was a dark wanton, man, ere she came to bed to either of us. Still sullen? Why, then, what a base fellow art thou, that wouldst leave thy father the butcher to be a poet, and have a patron, and write him modern verses an he were thy Ganymede: and yet knowest no better than to make a great matter betwixt gentlemen of a night's foining with a woman coloured ill! You make me [*coughing: weak, desperate*] — you make me laugh . . . Master Will.

TUTOR. What a world of buried wickedness is here! I will again assay to bring his mind to prayer.

LORD. Wait! I would ask him something. Was it your poet-tutor, or tutor-poet, friend, whom you wronged after this fashion? And had you his forgiveness? Was there reconciliation betwixt you?

OLD MAN. Trouble me not . . . I have no memory. [*Agitated*] I say, do not trouble me. . . . But, yes: I had his forgiveness —for that and other matters. He could not help himself. He loved me.

LORD. [*softly*] Loved you!

OLD MAN. Or the divine idea of me, he would say. Plato, one of your plaguey Athenians, was ruler in such matters in those days. And right burdensome was it, I do avouch to thee, thus to be laid up by a most voluble rhymer in this same Plato's Elysium! These sonnets, mark you, were passing current among our private friends. What between that, and the pestilent dark wanton (who downright frightened me e'en as I tumbled her, green lad that I was), and my mother's still urging on me plain Mistress Jane, our neighbour's daughter: with all that, can you wonder that I ran away to sea?

LORD. Ran away to sea! You are a sailor?

OLD MAN. [*offended*] I am a gentleman, as I have before declared to you. But for some months I was at sea; and at a glorious time. It was in eighty-eight, myself being then a lad of sixteen years.

LORD. [*awed*] In eighty-eight! You are one of those that sailed against the mighty Armada of Philip of Spain!

OLD MAN. That am I, truly.

LORD. Not under . . . not under Sir Francis Drake?

OLD MAN. [*offended again*] Marry nay, forsooth. Under the Lord High Admiral himself: a kinsman (and that at not more than five removes) of my ever-to-be honoured mother.

LORD. Is not this a wonder, Master Neville?

TUTOR. Every old dog has had his day, my lord. . . . And you were in action, friend, against that horned moon of mighty ships?

OLD MAN. That was I, indeed. And a right deadly, mortal moon it was — as my poet, indeed, was presently to call it. I was in action and believed killed — and then discharged honourably and so home again. And a fine bother was made of me. My late tutor

forgot his black wanton for a time and hymned me famously. I
would you could hear him now.

POET'S VOICE [*preternatural, remote — since this is a triumphant
sonnet and the climax of the piece: but this of course holds in some
measure of these irruptions throughout*]

> Not mine own fears, nor the prophetic soul
> Of the wide world dreaming on things to come,
> Can yet the lease of my true love control,
> Suppos'd as forfeit to a confin'd doom.
> The mortal moon hath her eclipse endur'd,
> And the sad augurs mock their own presage;
> Incertainties now crown themselves assur'd,
> And peace proclaims olives of endless age.
> Now with the drops of this most balmy time
> My love looks fresh, and Death to me subscribes,
> Since, spite of him, I'll live in this poor rhyme,
> While he insults o'er dull and speechless tribes:
> > And thou in this shalt find thy monument,
> > When tyrants' crests and tombs of brass are spent.

LORD. [*the poet's voice having gone out on echo*] Hear him now? I
think I almost can. . . . But do not you judge that the old man
mends, Neville? This talk of war has rallied him.

TUTOR. It is but a flicker of flame, I fear me, in what must soon be
ashes cold enough. See, his eyes close again, and the crippled
fingers of these once fine hands fumble and pluck. I doubt there
will be little more but impertinency from him now.

OLD MAN. *Tempus*, Master Will . . . *tempus*? Why, *singulariter,
nominativo, tempus*, time. *Rerum*, genitive case plural: *singulariter,
nominativo, res*, thing. *Edax* is hard. . . . Devourer, you
say? Then I have it. *Tempus edax rerum*: time, devourer of
things. [*Impatient*] But I care not for this *edax rerum*. Now, can I
go play?

POET'S VOICE. [*coming in on echo, clear for a moment, and then fading
again on echo: elegiac throughout*]

> . . . And Time that gave doth now his gift confound.
> Time doth transfix the flourish set on youth,
> And delves the parallels in beauty's brow,
> Feeds on the rarities of Nature's truth,
> And nothing stands but for his scythe to mow:
> > And yet to times in hope my verse shall stand,
> > Praising thy worth, despite his cruel hand.

TUTOR. Shortly before dawn came the physician who did then attend upon his majesty's ambassador in that place. There was little he could do for our dying countryman. He grew weaker: his mind still wandering and his speech but a drift of words out of some world of folly long gone by. But ever and again he would seem to fall upon a certain further discourse of rhyme, with a mumbling of verses, innocent indeed, but full of a rusty Elizabethanism (as a man might say) and such as, being altogether profane, little sorted with the stance of one who should presently bow his knees to judgement. My young lord nevertheless, although his due prayers and pious ejaculations were not wanting on the old man's behalf, did greatly wonder at this same rubble and mere *detritus* of poesy, and would decline his ear even so low as the dying man's pallet, the better to hear the same.

OLD MAN. [*whisper*] Beauty o'ersnowed and bareness everywhere.

LORD. Didst thou hear, Neville? [*Continues haltingly, as if piecing together what he has just heard:*]
      For never-resting Time leads summer on
      To hideous winter and confounds him there,
      Sap check'd with frost and lusty leaves quite gone,
      Beauty o'ersnowed and bareness everywhere. . . .
Friend . . . friend, do you hear me? Your tutor, he that made you those verses, what did they call him?

OLD MAN. Will.

LORD. Aye — Will, indeed. And what more? Would I had his verses in my cabinet!

OLD MAN. Say you? What more? Nay, I know not. I remember not. Nor no man else, either, I judge. He was a butcher's boy, whose parts for a time raised him to decent station in my father's household. But he sank again — and to lower than the low. He became, men said, a common player.

LORD. A player? But his name, man! Will —— ?

OLD MAN. [*very weak, but not beyond irritation*] I tell you, he had none. He was not as I, my lord, the bearer of a name not less honourable . . . mark you . . . not less honourable than that . . . than that of any gentleman in our shire: a *lasting* name. . . . Oh . . . oh! [*Dies*].

TUTOR. He has gone, my lord.

LORD. Then, God rest his soul! But his poet: I would fain have
known his poet's name.

TUTOR. It were more convenient, my lord, to know his own,
so that his grave be not without all memorial, or his burial
unbeseeming whatever quality was his. But he has been
known in this wretched place, it seems, only as *il Inglese*; and
he is without possessions.

LORD. Except his dial. Find it, Neville. His father gave it him.
It should be not without his name, or at least his arms.

TUTOR. I have it. Hold the taper closer, my lord. Yes! There is
something, although almost worn away, on the back hereof.

LORD. A name?

TUTOR. Only a cipher, my lord, as of two letters intertwined:
W. H.

Oxford and North Oxford

IN THE OPENING sentence of *Death at the President's Lodging* Dr Johnson is recalled as having observed that an academic life puts one little in the way of extraordinary casualties. This certainly held true for me during the 25 years I spent at Christ Church. The Queen came and opened something, but there was nothing out of the way about that. Two of the dons hit out at one another (were, as a colleague put it, at jar together and by the ears) in the senior common room, but I missed this, and it was only a few days' wonder anyway. A pupil of mine was theatened with solemn penalties because he preferred being married to living in sin. Charlie Chaplin came to dinner and made a polished speech in Received Standard English. I myself practised for weeks a speech which had to begin, 'Mr Chancellor, Mr Vice-Chancellor, your Excellencies, my Lord Archbishop, your Grace, my Lords, and Gentlemen' (or something of that sort), without any craven glancing at a note.

There were small events, too, in the university at large. André Gide, coming to Oxford accompanied by a young friend to receive an honorary degree, and asked whether there was anything he would particularly like to see, opted for the rooms in Magdalen College of his old friend Oscar Vild. Expecting something little short of a shrine, he was astounded at being ushered into an apartment in the temporary occupancy of the college rugger club, which was conducting an orgiastic binge there, with much Fescinnine song. E. M. Forster visited the Oxford Playhouse to witness the *première* of a dramatic version of *A Passage to India*. Sitting, for some reason, dwarfed between two giants, he kept on peeping round to assure himself that we were all enjoying the play as much as he was. (That was in January 1960. Later that year, I was to be introduced to him at a party celebrating, among other things, his most famous public appearance: as a witness in the affair of Lady Chatterley.) At about the same time there was a visit by an author eminent in a different branch of literature: Georges Simenon, the creator of Maigret. This was a publisher's jaunt, and included a luncheon party at what was still the Mitre Hotel. Enid Starkie, an exceedingly colourful Modern Languages don, so dominated the occasion that Simenon's unobtrusive disappearance from it passed undetected for quite some time. A couple of hours later, he was discovered standing at Carfax, watching people go by. Coming away from this affair, I was buttonholed by a hall porter, who expatiated enthusiastically on my talents. I was naturally gratified by this, but presently I became aware of a puzzling unfamiliarity in the titles he cited. He was confusing me with another Mr Innes, one of much wider acclaim.

We lived in North Oxford, in a house rented from Christ Church. Not all our neighbours were dons, but nearly all were in one way or another alarmingly distinguished. My wife, although not much given to deferential attitudes, was almost awed on realizing that our nearest neighbour was a certain Robert McCarrison, who had revolutionized an entire field of medicine. The McCarrisons were elderly and childless, and they doted — but particularly Sir Robert himself doted — on children. Unfortunately their conception of childhood, and of proper childhood behaviour, was based upon such children as they had been permitted to read about in their Victorian nurseries. North Oxford children, being brought up on enlightened modern principles, are for the most part atrociously wicked. So children's parties at the McCarrisons — particularly at Christmas when some quintessentially demonic infant would infallibly be chosen to hand round the little presents from the tree — were occasions of considerable anxiety to parents.

Almost opposite the McCarrisons lived Air Vice-Marshal Foster Macneice-Foster, who had been some kind of adviser to Chiang Kai-shek. The AVM was a most clubbable and indeed convivial man, whose presence at High Table and in common room at Christ Church was highly prized by us all. He drove himself round in an old car which, although its collisions had been in the main with prosaic pillar-boxes and lamp-posts, bore the appearance of having been much battered by tanks in the Western Desert. I recall an occasion upon which he drove me back from college to North Oxford after dining with us. There seemed to be a marked paucity of other traffic on the streets, and this puzzled me until I observed that every intersection was manned by a policeman. This civic courtesy (as it was) the AVM later repaid by serving for a term of years as Oxford's Lord Mayor.

Another alarming person to be driven through Oxford by was Professor Lord David Cecil, a further close neighbour. Unlike the AVM's, his pace was never other than sedate. But that he was at the wheel of a moving vehicle by no means inhibited his favourite mannerism of linking his fingers and with amazing rapidity twiddling his thumbs. As he drove, moreover, he talked eagerly and charmingly, courteously holding the gaze of his interlocutor the while, and with no regard whatever for such circumambient traffic as there might be. Just so must it have been when his governess allowed him to take the reins of a pony-cart in the unpeopled immensities of the park of Hatfield House.

That David Cecil was our neighbour for a time arose from the fact that he was indeed a professor. Fellows of colleges could live where they chose; professors of the university were under the stern necessity of having their dwellings within (I think) three and a half miles of Carfax. Cecil, holding a fellowship at New College and becoming aware of a professorship looming up, hastened to buy himself a house in the Cotswolds, trusting that the university would sufficiently honour his attachment to the land to abrogate its requirement in his favour. The university, however, proved adamant, and he had to buy a small house in Charlbury Road. In this matter he was less fortunate, or less ingenious, than another of our neighbours for a time. He was a professor of mathematics who, having had enough of Oxford suburban life, hit upon the plan of having his wife inherit an important herd of pedigree cattle. These creatures he was presently able to represent as miserably bellowing and mooing in trucks which had conveyed them to Oxford railway station. Impressed by this bovine plight, the university gave way at once, and the professor, like some biblical patriarch, folded his North Oxford tents and departed with his wife, family and cattle to fitter pastures elsewhere. But in Oxford he did, at least, retain a Chair.

There was, as it happened, a small herd of dairy cattle at our back door. It was conducted on hyper-hygienic principles by an octogenarian lady, Kathleen Haldane, and we all had to get our milk from her. Mrs Haldane was the widow of J. S. Haldane, the

eminent physiologist, and mother of J. B. S. Haldane, the almost
equally eminent geneticist. Her house, with grounds which ran
down to the Cherwell, had a large open hall and staircase
distinguished by a collection of signed photographs on the walls
which constituted a kind of history of European science over
many decades. For some years we kept a dinghy in Mrs Haldane's
boat-house, and to reach it had to pass the windows of what had
been the senior Professor Haldane's private laboratory. From its
rafters there perplexingly depended a somewhat rusty push-bike.
It turned out to be the forerunner of all those contraptions for
enjoying cycling exercise while staying put which one now sees
advertised in magazines. J. S. Haldane had a famous fancy for
being his own guinea-pig, and was particularly interested in the
effect of continued exertion amid mounting levels of carbon
dioxide. The bike had been used for experiments in conditions of
that sort.

It was in the grounds of this house — and I think when Mrs
Haldane was alone in it — that there occurred the only suggestion
of hostilities that Oxford was to know during the Second World
War. Suddenly there had been a tremendous explosion. Mrs
Haldane had said to herself, 'enemy action', armed herself with a
revolver, and gone out to cope with the situation. What had
happened was something like this: the pilot of a friendly aircraft
— perhaps a Pole — had got into trouble over North Oxford, and
had avoided disaster on the crowded playing-fields of a preparatory school only by crashing his plane on the cottage of Mrs
Haldane's chauffeur. The pilot was, I suppose, killed, but the
cottage was fortunately unoccupied, perhaps because the chauffeur had been called to the colours long before. Mrs Haldane,
although an ardent patriot, is said to have been outraged at Mr
Churchill's having failed to order the immediate restoration of
the cottage.

Both J. S. Haldane and his elder brother Richard (who was to
become Lord Chancellor of England as Viscount Haldane of
Cloan, and be aspersed as 'pro-German' at the time of the Kaiser's
War) were Edinburgh Academy boys. Richard is on record as
having disliked the school. Possibly he had there encountered
somebody like Buckie Green.

Of literary people there weren't many immediately around.
An exception was Anne Bridge, the author of *Peking Picnic* and
other novels. She was in fact the wife of a retired ambassador,

Owen O'Malley, who regarded his own career as having been a failure and was probably no great admirer of hers. They were, however, an entertaining as well as a devoted couple, and for years we saw more of them than of any other of our neighbours. Our intimacy was the easier in that I had never read any of Lady O'Malley's novels, nor she any of mine. She liked to be addressed as 'Bridge', and she had a good deal to say about royalty-rates and (generally on a complaining note) reviews. Owen O'Malley occasionally betrayed wider literary interests (as well as intellectual ones). He had an amusing anecdote of his attempt as a young man to pay a visit to Thomas Hardy at Max Gate. The front door was opened to him by a 'snivelling slut' who met his application with a firm rejection, a little softened by the words, 'Poor Mr Hardy, 'e do have a right terrible cold again.' Wystan Auden had better luck on that doorstep many years later.

North Oxford, then, although much celebrated by the muse of John Betjeman, was undistinguished in terms of literary eminence. It quite failed to compete with Boars Hill to the south of the city, which had, successively or simultaneously, harboured Robert Bridges, Gilbert Murray, John Masefield, and Robert Graves. I set eyes, I believe, on all of these, but met only Murray — having been taken to a tea-time call on him by a Christ Church don old enough to have been his colleague in the college during his long tenure of the Regius Professorship of Greek. Although austere and sad, Professor Murray was infinitely courteous, and had, I believe, taken the trouble to look into *Death at the President's Lodging* for the occasion. Only once or twice did he have to control a flicker of impatience; it was when his splendid wife, whose memory had entirely crumbled in old age, asked me three or four times in as many minutes whether I would take another cup of tea. Murray fascinated me on three distinct accounts. He was reported to be the original of Cusins in Bernard Shaw's *Major Barbara*. He was the author of those translations of Greek drama which Sybil Thorndike had brought alive for me on the stage as a boy. And I had heard in common room several accounts of his having exhibited there certain very odd powers of mind. He would be sent from the room. Somebody would secrete a banknote within the pages of one of the many books shelved on the walls. Murray would return, and slowly but with certainty make his way to it. Whether he could have done so without the presence of some twenty people determined *not* to afford him any

Above: The family
in 1952

Left: JIMS in 1950

Three generations, 1964

John and Margaret in Rome for a wedding

A family composed . . . and discomposed (1974)

In the cloister, Christ Church

help, I don't know. The kind of hyperaesthesia which would thus explain the feat is held to be not altogether uncommon. It was said, however, that Murray and a daughter could place themselves in telepathic communication when at a considerable remove from each other, at least in their own house. But I recall no direct testimony about this.

I return to North Oxford, where I was remarking on the paucity of literati. The situation changed, however, as soon as one had crossed the University Parks (a single park perplexingly so named until one learnt that lines of artillery had stood in it during the Civil War). For overlooking this area, and close to Keble College, was the home of Joyce Cary, Oxford's only recorded resident major novelist, so to speak, until the emergence into prominence of Miss Iris Murdoch round about the time of Cary's death. Cary led, in his own words, 'a very retired life, not because I don't like company, but because I have a lot of work to do.' His methods of working, which are now fairly well known, indeed involved him in prodigious labour, and also to the accumulation in attic rooms of what textual critics call 'foul papers' in fantastic abundance. By 'company' he probably meant a small evening gathering of friends in his own house on something like a weekly basis. As no more than a slender acquaintance, I attended these meetings only on two or three occasions, and I remember little about them. My one extended conversation with Cary took place on a late-night train from London to Oxford — on that same Fornicator, indeed, on which, a few years later, I was to experience misgivings over Ernest Jones's possible response to *The Hawk and the Handsaw*.

We had both attended — I think at the Savoy — the *dîner Molière*, a function at which the then French ambassador, a genial Corsican, entertained writers on a scale which put the entire literary establishment (as it was beginning to be called) of the metropolis awesomely on view. Now, alone in a compartment with Cary, I soon felt that I was taking the minor rôle in something like one of my own Imaginary Conversations for Rayner Heppenstall. Cary told me, among other things, that never in his life had he invented anything. He even seemed to suggest that it would be positively immoral in anybody to attempt to do so. Everything in his books had actually *happened* before his eyes, and he had been able to chronicle them as copiously as he had done because he possessed in notable degree the power of total recall.

Having read all Cary's novels up to that date, I did my best to think about this. *Mister Johnson*, yes — and indeed perhaps all the African books. But *Charley is my Darling*: how could he, in any sense, have *witnessed* that? Was he talking for effect? Decidedly he was not. Was he kidding himself? He was obviously a clear-headed man. Nor had the excellence of the ambassador's wine anything to do with it. Joyce Cary was entirely sober, and being good enough to talk to me as writer to writer. Spending six or seven weeks of every year, as I did, desperately *inventing* exploits for John Appleby, I was bewildered by this setting of memory at a premium. But I had to admit to myself that I had been listening, broadly, to something essentially true.

There is an ironic sequel to this mystery. The trilogy ending with *The Horse's Mouth*, and with it the career of Gulley Jimson, was already several years behind Cary, *when Gulley Jimson turned up on him*. The door-bell in Parks Road rang; Cary himself answered it — and there stood Gulley: a needy artist come home. Oxford is rather good at inventing stories with a spark of wit to them. But this story is true. And Cary did everything he could for the real-life Gulley, who had thus, if belatedly, *happened before his eyes*. Here and there about Oxford he got the man commissions. His paintings, although not quite up to those of the Jimson of the books, may still be seen in more than one senior common room.

Seattle and Point-No-Point

EIGHT MODERN WRITERS was ready to go to the press in 1960, and the material I had gathered for it enabled me to survive for some months as a visiting professor in the University of Washington at Seattle. The academic community there proved warmly and abundantly hospitable, and I retain an uneasy feeling that I didn't do too well in it. Party-giving apart, the main activities appeared to be delivering and attending lectures (they began, I seem to recall, at 8 a.m.) and cheering on a team of footballers. My own conception of a lecture was of a discourse polished to a quite unnecessary degree, with — so to speak — every comma in its right place, and by the time I was managing this five days a week for some weeks on end, it was my feeling that the place was getting its money's worth. I therefore tended to retire to my typewriter and Michael Innes. My wife, although (as was her habit) she made a few acquaintances who were to turn up and be received as established friends elsewhere and later on, put in a good deal of time reading *Clarissa*.

Seattle, like Vancouver to the north of it, is a beautifully situated city, agreeably up-and-down, and with complicated inlets of the Pacific Ocean peeping from the end of many of its streets. It also possesses a national park in which, no more than 40 or 50 miles away, there is a magic mountain. Mount Rainier can only be called that. Visible from the windows of our apartment hotel, it was seldom where it had been a few hours before. It approached; it withdrew; sometimes even (it seemed to me) it moved from quarter to quarter of the horizon. All this, no doubt, was a phenomenon obeying atmospheric laws. But it was as mysterious as the floating island of Aeolus in the *Odyssey*, and we took endless delight in it.

Of the scores of professors met in Seattle, I remember most clearly the poet Theodore Roethke. He taught creative writing, and took immense pains in selecting his pupils from among the swarms who sought selection, with some satisfactory results as a consequence. He was, however, of melancholic temperament and (as it was to prove) in the penultimate year of his life. About the feasibility and utility of bringing imaginative literature — whether it be poetry, prose, fiction, or drama — within the *atelier* system long established in the fields of music and the plastic arts, I have to be content to bear an open mind. No experience of anything of the sort has ever come my way.

We made several expeditions from Seattle. Two were to Vancouver, and the first of these was to give a lecture at the University of British Columbia, an institution most agreeably mingling American and British academic customs. I recall, however, the chill horror of suddenly being called upon for extemporary speech at a large party conducted upon strictly no-alcohol-on-campus principles. Disconcerting, too, was being accommodated in a guest-suite so lavishly supplied with electric gadgetry that the very bedclothes crackled with static at a touch. Rashly, and supposing all to be far from well, I raised an alarm about this, and suffered the mortification of being treated as one virtually strayed out of Noah's ark. Our second visit was merely in the interest of exploration. We crossed to Vancouver Island, and drove north from the little town of Victoria, not without hope of coming upon a grizzly bear. (The creatures were said to come nuzzling at trash-cans exposed outside isolated dwellings.)

There was certainly plenty of isolation. The greater part of Vancouver Island appeared virtually devoid of human habitation. I had inquired, not very hopefully, about the possibility of somewhere obtaining a meal, and had been told that something of the kind might conceivably be had at Point-No-Point. Point-No-Point, it seems, is simply a term drawn from the science of navigation, but I was obscurely disturbed by it — and for this I believe I later found a reason in a rereading of the Elizabethan dramatist, Thomas Kyd:

> Oh, world! No world, but mass of public wrong,
> Confused and filled with murder and misdeeds!

World-No-World, Point-No-Point. We drove on, with nothing much ahead of us in any way notable, it seemed, short of the North Pole. If a bear should turn up, it would be polar and not grizzly. But eventually we did come upon Point-No-Point. It was a modest little dwelling, and on the very verge of the Pacific Ocean. It must have had windows looking straight at Japan.

We made our application, and were handed a sketch-plan of the immediate surroundings, told to wander around for half an hour, and then return for luncheon. This we did. The meal proved to be very French. So French was it, indeed, that only in such rarely visited places as, say, the Barrier in Tours have I met its like. One knows that in Quebec one can turn a corner and step into France. One may be a little surprised to find in Montreal a predominantly French-speaking city rather larger than Paris. But to find a three-star French restaurant at Point-No-Point is distinctly astonishing. It stretches the term 'French-Canadian' very far indeed.

We returned to Victoria, and must have spent two or three nights there, since it was late one evening that it, too, sprang a surprise on us. The extent of the surprise requires a word about the city, which may be described as the nearest thing to Cheltenham that the western hemisphere affords. Moreover, Victoria is a *Victorian* city. It is full of English people who have their roots essentially in that age, and its municipality has striven to make them feel at home even to the extent of having imported (surely at considerable expense) superannuated English lamp-posts. Nothing more decorous in the way of street-scenes could be conceived. But one of these streets was the setting for the only full-scale mugging I have ever witnessed. It was a wide street near the centre of the town, and the hour, I suppose, was one at which there weren't many people around. We suddenly saw, some fifteen yards ahead of us, a man huddled on the pavement, and three other men savagely kicking him wherever they could land a boot. We had scarcely taken in this extraordinary scene when a police-car appeared advancing rapidly towards us. My wife dashed into the street and attempted to flag it down. It swept past unregarding. Then the three assailants stopped their kicking and simply walked away. The man they had been attacking got to his feet and walked — or staggered — away too. The incident was concluded. Nobody to whom we reported it was at all surprised. Yes, they said, it was a season at which casual labourers tended to drift into the city from the rural areas. An urban environment was easier for them when unemployed. And some, of course, were rough types.

We travelled home by way of San Francisco, Miami, and Jamaica — being, I suppose, resolved to see something of the western hemisphere at large. San Francisco proved to be like Seattle, but with more emphasis on astonishment and a grand scale. There was the tremendous bridge, inexhaustibly astounding to the view. The streets swept up and down tremendous slopes, and went in for the same kind of cable trams as did the Edinburgh of my childhood. The campus at Berkeley, although it is no more than one of numerous institutions constituting the University of California, is nothing if not generously conceived. Our host there, Willard Farnham, although he had been Berkeley's senior Professor of English for many years, seemed sometimes uncertain of his bearings as he drove us around it. Of him and his wife, Fern, we had already seen much on more than one of their visits to Oxford. Both were scholars. Fern, much given to travel pursued in the interest of cultural improvement, was always wholly serious. She later published a definitive biography of Madame Dacier, who had also been a scholar married to a scholar, and who translated both the *Iliad* and the *Odyssey* into French prose at the close of the seventeenth century. Willard, possibly the most distinguished Shakespeare scholar in America, was less reliable in the matter of sober demeanour. When, on one occasion, we had taken the Farnhams to look at Cliveden, Fern addressed herself with appropriate severity to a careful inspection of the mansion. Willard, as a citizen of the great republic, was unimpressed by the spectacle of dollars by the million poured into the place in quest of senseless splendour, and slightly offended his wife by making too evident to other pilgrims an element of the sardonic in his regard.

After the Farnhams at Berkeley the dolphins at Miami. The ancients believed the dolphin to be a fish — and moreover regarded the dolphin as the king of the fish, as the lion is king of the beasts and the eagle of the birds. All these regal creatures can be 'tamed'. As a boy I must have seen a lion-tamer at work in a circus, and only recently I saw an eagle that had been conditioned, like a falcon, to return to the lure. Dolphins, a popular encyclopaedia tells me, 'can be taught complex tricks and are frequently exhibited for public amusement'. At Miami there is a large amphitheatre equipped for this amusement. We attended it, and saw the creatures put through their tricks. Only, and precisely, it wasn't like that at all. Despite all that the dolphins did (and they could do things beyond amazement), what we were present at was less an entertainment than a mystery in the antique and august sense of the word. The dolphins, although living not even in the same medium as man, overpoweringly suggested themselves as our closest kin in all the width and depth of creation: thinking as well as sentient beings, with whom it ought to be possibly not merely to sport but also to confer. The men and women in charge of them seemed aware of this, comporting themselves with the gravity of scientists in a laboratory rather than with the boredom of keepers in a zoo. One suspected, nevertheless, that somebody was making a good deal of money out of the dolphins.

From Miami on to Jamaica, where some Oxford connection had secured us for a few weeks the loan of a house some fifteen miles east of Montego Bay. Arriving at Kingston and hiring a car, we drove across the breadth of the island to our destination. As observed on this occasion, Jamaica seemed populated solely by wandering and enormous black men, all nearly naked, and all carrying correspondingly naked and enormous cutlasses. It was almost alarming. But the weapons, it seemed, were simply for chopping down clumps of bananas, which were everywhere to be had for the taking; and the rural populace was so law-abiding and right-thinking that small white children could take a tent or sleeping-bag and spend a tranquil night anywhere. The small white children probably came from big white houses sparingly and unostentatiously sited beside a private beach. The house lent to us was rather like that, and seemed commodious until there came the sudden news that the owners with their children, dogs, and servants were coming to join us after all. We had ourselves been joined at Miami by our youngest son, who had been in Mexico, and it was suggested that he should now sleep in a hammock at the bottom of the garden. This would have been an excellent arrangement (he certainly wouldn't have been alarmed by an occasional visit by a black man with a cutlass) but for the fact that some sort of rainy season appeared to have set in. I then discovered, however, that just beyond a beautiful stretch of water called, I think, Frenchmen's Cove there was a convenient hotel, and we went across to book our son in on a bed-and-breakfast basis. We had to go no further than a small lodge, where a dazzlingly beautiful Creole girl explained herself as in charge of the whole concern. The arrangement was made without difficulty. I did, however, think it prudent to fix a price, so I asked whether 35 shillings a night would be about right. At this my wife said very promptly, 'Thirty shillings', and by means of a small and graceful gesture the Creole girl accepted the entire adequacy of this. So 30 shillings was what our son paid. But his mere bathroom — or so he reported — was about the size of Buckingham Palace, and there later transpired the odd circumstance that the hotel was among the most expensive in all the Americas. It would fly you to and from New York any day of the week without extra payment, and simply as one of the courtesies of the house.

Fredericton

IN THE AUTUMN of 1962 I returned to Canada, this time on my own, making what was no more than a brief visit to the University of New Brunswick at Fredericton. I was there as the guest of Lord Beaverbrook.

This calls for brief explanation. Lord Beaverbrook was fond of giving himself out as a New Brunswick boy (actually, he was born in Ontario) and one of his means to declaring this piety had been to take over the university. Virtually, at least, it came to that, and for some years he had vindicated the rôle by arriving for a few weeks every October and occupying the official residence of the President — who, for the duration of the visit, had to shift for himself. Recently, however, Beaverbrook had presented Fredericton with a picture gallery in memory of his wife, and in part of this building had treated himself to a suite of rooms more than adequate for a brief residence with a small entourage. (In the gallery itself I recall only a portrait of the donor by Graham Sutherland, one of the artist's characteristically disobliging things: the sitter — or squatter — something resembling a toad preserved in liquor within a sealed glass jar.)

During these visits the Chancellor (for Beaverbrook of course was that) supplied the university with a visiting academic person, who gave a short course of lectures and was awarded an honorary degree for his pains. This was how I came to be in Fredericton. A. J. P. Taylor, a close friend and later the biographer of Beaverbrook, had been my immediate predecessor, and as my own close friend had obviously drafted me in. My successor was, I think, Dr A. L. Rowse. An Imaginary Conversation between Dr Rowse and his lordship could be quite something.

Fredericton proved to be *very* dry. At Seattle, indeed, no liquor could be bought at any point within a couple of miles of the campus. But Fredericton was much drier than that. In an obscure quarter of the city, indeed, there was a small shop — got up with a red light over the door as if to suggest a brothel — where I was told a bottle of gin might be bought. But of course I was much too shy to attempt that. When the President of the university gave a sherry-party — as he occasionally did — it had to be behind carefully lowered blinds. Even if one went out to dine in a hotel, one had to get through several substantial courses by way of establishing one's bona fides as a legitimate claimant for a half-bottle of wine. This, however, is by the way, and accounts for no part of my interest and pleasure on discovering that I had a standing invitation to dine with Beaverbrook in his private establishment. I did so on half a dozen occasions.

He was an admirable host — the more remarkably so in that he was frequently (it could just be detected) in great pain. (He died within a couple of years of these encounters.) He could, indeed, suddenly become very angry in a manner I found slightly alarming on what were, with a single exception, tête-à-tête occasions. He was furious with me when I betrayed wholly inadequate knowledge in the field of cheeses. He was much more furious on recalling that a royal personage had lately turned a fire-hose on a group of journalists. But about this he remained clear-headed. The unforgivable thing, he said, was that the men thus drenched were unable to hit back.

On the single night on which there was other company Beaverbrook was a curiously changed man. Two lumber-tycoons (as I thought of them) had come to dinner, and their host, who with me had been both amusing and disposed to be amused, discussed lumber with gravity and a contented provinciality. How a good yoke of bullocks at Stamford fair? It was rather like that, if on a larger scale. This mischievous old man had become for the occasion indistinguishable from a sober merchant prince in *Buddenbrooks*. Each of the tycoons, incidentally, had brought a son with him: young men of perhaps eighteen or nineteen, students at the university. Were they to have wine? Our host put the question to their fathers. No, decidedly not. The young men themselves produced gestures or murmurs disclaiming any acquaintance with wine. Beer, perhaps? The fathers pronounced with equal decision against that. And again their sons took pains to agree. At the end of the evening the two fathers drove away — whether separately or together, I don't know — and Lord Beaverbrook's own car was summoned to return the two sons to their hall of residence. Walking back to my own quarters, I found myself puzzling over this small episode. I had to conclude that in

Canada a heavy paternalism must obtain, and that our host had remembered the fact as he remembered everything else.

A few days later I was flown to Montreal in an aeroplane I judged to be surprisingly small until I discovered I was the only passenger. And even high over the Atlantic that night I hadn't quite escaped from the Beaverbrook level of things, which in this instance meant much proffering of champagne, and an enormous breakfast some two hours (as it seemed) after an enormous dinner. The University of New Brunswick also did me proud, presenting me with six tumblers embellished with the university arms, together with a bottle of whisky. When at Heathrow I had to pay duty on the whisky (since a half-bottle was all I'd have been allowed to take in free), I almost expected an emissary of his lordship to advance with a hand in his pocket and settle the matter.

Michael Innes (5) Hare Sitting Up

DURING THESE YEARS Michael Innes remained steadily productive — so productive, indeed, as to make it appear almost certain that he must be repeating himself. Consider, for instance, *Hare Sitting Up*, published in 1959, and which I have just reread. The title-page explains itself thus:

> You yourself, don't you find it a beautiful
> clean thought, a world empty of people, just
> uninterrupted grass, and a hare sitting up?
>
> D. H. LAWRENCE, *Women in Love*

So — I tell myself — there is to be that strong literary garnish again. I turn a few pages, and find that we are going to have dealings with identical twins! It is a means to comical confusion at least as old as Plautus. And have I not had recourse to them before — perhaps back in 1948, in *A Night of Errors*? I have a look at that earlier story, and am relieved. It certainly concerns a family of Dromios, who through some centuries, however, have gone in not for twins but for triplets. And out of my Dromio triplets a great deal of farce is extracted. So here *Hare Sitting Up* escapes the charge of being *crambe repetita*. But now it appears that one of my twins is a scientist; that he is possibly a mad scientist; that conceivably he is roaming the land with a culture of almost inconceivable virulence in his pocket! There is no escaping here the charge of cauld kail het again. In common with almost every thriller-writer in the land, I have set this wandering Thanatos on my stage before.

Yet the components of *Hare Sitting Up*, although all too familiar, are deployed with what strikes me now as considerable virtuosity. The key to the whole affair — a key which Appleby senses to be not turning in its lock because of some elusive failure of his ear somewhere early in the action — lies in the fact that a fairly common English Christian name is also a common noun, and moreover starts off like a possessive pronoun. So much for routine ingenuity. The conversations, whether of small boys at a private school, newly graduated Oxford students on a railway train, devoted ornithologists, or persons represented as carrying grave responsibilities for the safety of the state, are unobtrusively equivocal at need, as well as adequately lively and verisimilar throughout. And the 'literary' flavour reflects something quite genuine. The ghost of Thomas Love Peacock occasionally breathes in the talk; and the characterization, if sketchy, is by somebody who has rejoiced in Charles Dickens long ago.

Hare Sitting Up isn't too bad. Yet as the story moves towards its conclusion I find myself increasingly impatient with it. Sustained suspense, and puzzlement maintained up to the very last moment, are too much at a premium. They squeeze any illusion of real life out of the thing, so that I have nothing but puppets on which to bring down the curtain.

But here I am quarrelling with the necessary limitations of a minor literary kind. The complex mystery story is irreconcilable with any authentic representative fiction, and peculiarly so with the traditional amplitude of the English novel. Anthony Trollope in his *Autobiography* has a criticism of Wilkie Collins which is relevant here:

> I can never lose the taste of the construction. The author seems always to be warning me to remember that something happened at exactly half-past two o'clock on Tuesday morning; or that a woman disappeared from the road just fifteen yards beyond the fourth milestone.

To reconcile in a single story milestones that are numerous and important with the leisured portrayal for its own sake of a group of characters or a social scene, requires, we may think, an artistry worthy of higher things. Almost invariably such an effort must fail. Either the mystery will appear paltry (as did that of Dickens's Edwin Drood to George Gissing) or the alternative interests held out by the writer will be rejected as ungrateful padding. And if the milestones compose but ill into the panoramic novel, they are veritable millstones round the neck of any more elevated imaginative fiction.

The novelist always lurking in Michael Innes has coped with this situation as he can: preserving always a certain lightness of air in his writing: aerating it with such wit as he can command: escaping from the artificial into the fantastic or the farcical.

Yet as a literary kind the detective story, descended from the sensation novel at the end of the eighteenth century, has enjoyed an astonishingly long spell of public favour. There are aspects of it which deserve to be considered a little more at large.

Excursus on the Detective Story

IN THE OPENING chapter of *A Study in Scarlet* Dr Watson is introduced to Sherlock Holmes. Holmes says, 'How are you?', and adds: 'You have been in Afghanistan, I perceive.' Watson asks in astonishment: 'How on earth did you know that?' and Holmes, 'chuckling to himself', answers: 'Never mind.' In the following chapter the two men observe through a window 'a stalwart, plainly dressed individual' walking down the street with a letter in his hand. Watson says, 'I wonder what that fellow is looking for?' and Holmes says: 'You mean the retired sergeant of Marines.' In each instance Holmes details the observations and deductions leading to his conclusion, but he does so only after a more or less teasing delay. Watson, if a close observer, could have marked what was chiefly revealing in the Marine — notably, 'a great blue anchor tattooed on the back of the fellow's hand'. ('That smacked of the sea,' Holmes explained.) But we ourselves have not been allowed to note either this, or the military carriage, or the regulation side-whiskers, or 'some amount of self-importance and a certain air of command', or the manner in which the Marine held his head and swung his cane. As the Holmes saga developed, Conan Doyle came to see that it would be to the advantage of the stories that his readers should be afforded a glimpse of the clues as they turn up. But he sets no great emphasis on this. In the main, we simply follow Holmes around and admire in due season. There is no premium, such as there is in the developed detective story, on driving us to exclaim: 'I ought to have spotted *that!*'

Perhaps the most famous clue in the Holmes corpus is that afforded by the dog that did nothing in the night-time. But on the whole Holmes's clues are objects, particularly those that may be detected through a magnifying-glass: Holmes's glass is almost as famous as his deerstalker cap. Some of the clues, although solid, must be described as transparent too. There is often a largeness, as well as innocence, about these minutiae which corresponds to something in the personality of their creator and must be among the factors contributing to the enduring popularity of Holmes's investigations.

In all such stories the clues, if they are to be acceptable, must not be recondite: the last reaction to be desired in the reader is an indignant 'But I never knew that!' Thus a polymathic detective may prove a liability, and here Conan Doyle's initial conception of his hero was insufficiently considered. Holmes, it is true, is declared (absurdly) to be ignorant of Copernican astronomy, but he has a 'profound' knowledge of chemistry and has written a monograph discriminating the ashes of 140 varieties of tobacco. In *A Study in Scarlet* he knows that somebody has been smoking a Trichinopoly cigar, but since we have not read his monograph there is no possibility of our making the same identification and reasoning from it. Frequently Holmes has to explain to Watson the significance of matters which Watson, like ourselves, is not specialist enough to know anything about. Thus, in the same story, Holmes detects that a cab and not a private carriage has at one point been involved because of 'the narrow gauge of the wheels'. We are regularly and justly impressed by Holmes's powers of observation and inference. But there is no contest between ourselves and the detective, just as there seems to be none recorded between Holmes's prototype, Dr Joseph Bell, and his pupils in Edinburgh (or, indeed, between that *Ur*-Holmes, Voltaire's Zadig, and the authorities of Babylon in the mystery of the sacred horse of the king and the queen's respectable dog).

Clues, then, if they are to be fair, must fall within the area of common knowledge the validity of which a judge in court feels free to take into judicial notice: things so generally known to be true that evidence need not be led to validate them. So the writer becomes involved in matters of social tact, endeavouring to estimate the likely extent of his readers' acquirements. A great many people know that dentists commonly wear white jackets; a smaller but still substantial section of society has had the opportunity of observing that stewards on passenger aircraft are (or at one time were) similarly attired. Almost anybody of sufficient education to find the word 'haemophilia' even vaguely informative is aware that the blood of sufferers from the disease does not readily clot; and may even be able to recall, and grasp as relevant to the plot he is following, the fact that individuals descended from a particular European dynasty are, at least marginally, more likely to suffer from haemophilia than are the common run of us.

In the 100 years since the publication of *A Study in Scarlet* the detective story has developed a great deal, and notably in the ingeniously unobtrusive presentation of clues. The height of virtuosity here is achieved, I suppose, by the writer who gets such a clue into the title of a book, as does Agatha Christie in *Why Didn't They Ask Evans?*, or into the very first word of it (as I believe I have myself twice managed). It is Agatha Christie, too, who regularly contrives that just as the clue is dropped a distracting incident occurs. Here we are close to the art of the stage conjurer.

Again, over this long period of time the clue tends steadily to refine and even attenuate itself in consonance with the enhanced acuity of readers. It is no longer at all likely to be the imprint of a boot in the clayey soil. It may be no more than a nuance of speech. And here once more — rather surprisingly — Christie is supreme. Thus in what I take to be the most famous of developed detective novels, *The Murder of Roger Ackroyd*, Ackroyd's secretary hears his employer's voice coming from his study: '*The calls on my purse have been so frequent of late that I fear it is impossible for me to accede to your request.*'

Poirot sees that nobody would *talk* like this — except into a dictaphone. This is perhaps a surprising feat on Poirot's part, since he is a Belgian who consistently speaks a foreigner's stage English, and moreover is so linguistically uncertain that he has occasional difficulty with phrases imported from his own native French. But of course what Poirot here spots is true, and, if we have not remarked the fact as we read, it is for a reason taking us straight to the heart of Christie's mystery. Her writing is so flat and cliché-ridden and undistinguished that we pay very little regard to it as we forge through the story; if those phrases of Ackroyd's are oddly stiff it is just a matter of his creator's regrettable insufficiency in this important department of literature. Than this, however, nothing could be further from the truth. Christie commands, whenever she has need of it, a linguistic medium of quite astonishing finesse and subtlety. Indeed, in her mature novels the entire business of clues, narrowly regarded, becomes of secondary importance. The craft of the writer is directed predominantly to leading us into false assumptions by means of this virtuosity.

There are readers who dislike the technique, and speak of red herrings. Conan Doyle, in the last years of his life, may have been among those saddened that anybody should have written so outrageously immoral a book as *The Murder of Roger Ackroyd*. Take its mere opening paragraph:

> Mrs Ferrars died on the night of the 16th–17th September — a Thursday. I was sent for at eight o'clock on the morning of Friday the 17th. There was nothing to be done. She had been dead some hours.

And, a little further on, and from the same narrator, the similar precision of this:

> The letter had been brought in at twenty minutes to nine. It was just on ten minutes to nine when I left him, the letter still unread. I hesitated with my hand on the door handle, looking back and wondering if there was anything I had left undone. I could think of nothing. With a shake of the head I passed out and closed the door behind me.

If, having finished the book, one turns back to this, one is inclined to ask oneself whether stuff equally wicked, equally audacious, was ever penned. Is it surprising that, in the very year of the publication of *Ackroyd*, its author should have perpetrated an atrocious deceit involving the disappearance of her own person in an ostensibly amnesiac condition, so that hundreds of policemen and thousands of private individuals wasted a great deal of time going in search of her? The facts of that mysterious affair remain doubtful, and Mrs Christie may indeed have been very unwell. What is certain is that the chief delight of this in the main conventional upper-middle-class Englishwoman lay in foxing as many people as possible — and this eventually to the great content of millions. She could do it superbly either in novels or short stories. Consider one of the latter, 'The Red Signal', to be found in a collection called *The Agatha Christie Hour*.

A 'famous alienist' called Sir Alington West ('the supreme authority on mental disease', our apparently heavy-handed writer insists), together with his nephew, Dermot West, attend a dinner-party given by Jack Trent and his wife, Claire. Jack has 'a good-humoured smile and a pleasant lazy laugh'. Claire is tense and uneasy, so that Dermot (who is in love with her) concludes that she is going mad, and that his eminent uncle has been invited to the dinner by Jack in order covertly to diagnose her condition. Dermot goes home with his uncle, and they discuss the situation at considerable length. They then have a sudden, violent and not very plausible quarrel which is conveniently witnessed by a vastly stereotypic butler. Dermot goes on to a dance; returns at a late hour to his own flat; finds that a revolver has been planted among his handkerchiefs, and hard upon this learns that his uncle, the psychiatric Sir Alington, has been murdered.

And so on: it is all simple and absurd — but meanwhile we have been monstrously deceived. That long conversation between uncle and nephew has been so contrived as to conceal the fact that the interlocutors speak at cross-purposes throughout. A single 'he' or 'she' would give the game away, but it so happens that no single 'he' or 'she' is uttered. It is the husband (of the good-humoured smile and pleasant lazy laugh) and not the wife who is going mad and has been under Sir Alington's scrutiny at the dinner-party. And there has been a further authorial cunning. Between the dinner-party and the uncle-and-nephew dialogue we attend (somewhat inconsequently) a spiritualist seance at which everything said is suitably imbued with fogginess and ambiguity. After it, the crucial dialogue comes to us as crystal-clear, which is exactly what it is not. Stratagems of this reach and subtlety, boldy projected upon preposterous plots, are the staple of Agatha Christie's writing. They take us a long way from Conan Doyle.

Dorothy L. Sayers maintained that the essential rules for writing detective stores are laid down by Aristotle in the *Poetics*. Similarly, Ronald Knox professed to hold that, from *prooimion* to *epilogos*, such stories ought to be constructed on the model of Greek tragedy. There is something to be said for these learned thoughts. Aristotle declares that we, as children do, delight in imitation. If we reflect that every imitation is in some degree a deception, we must conclude that in deception, too, it is natural to delight: we enjoy being gulled. But curiosity, also, is native to us, and its gratification in the face of difficulty a triumph: there is thus satisfaction in an astounding *anagnorisis*. Agatha Christie's distinction lies in offering these allures in perfect balance. But they operate in a void. There is nothing else in the books. This was in the mind of Edmund Wilson when he wrote the formidable essay called 'Who cares who killed Roger Ackroyd?' We can only say that, within the limitations of a minor craft,

Agatha Christie could, at need, write with a verbal adroitness far exceeding anything that, in that craft, had gone before her.

But we have to note that, undeniably, Sherlock Holmes and his world are alive as Hercule Poirot and his world are not. Holmes has even entered the mythology of the folk, so that if in a pub a man is called 'a ruddy Sherlock Holmes' the expression is as generally understood as would be 'a bloody Shylock' or 'a regular Romeo'. But nobody has ever been called 'a peeping Poirot'. Why is this? Why is Baker Street as universally associated with Conan Doyle's hero as is Sherwood Forest with Robin Hood, or Greyfriars School with Billy Bunter? These are questions belonging to psychology and the study of archetypes.

The detective story has been with us sufficiently long to be of some interest, too, to the social historian, since the figure of the detective in popular fiction has evolved in terms of changing attitudes to the actual struggle against crime. The confusions and complexities of the eighteenth-century system of law-enforcement created in the lay mind a strong persuasion that thief-takers and criminals — cops and robbers, as they would now be called — were blood-brothers rather than enemies. The career of Jonathan Wild in England, the memoirs of Vidocq in France, William Godwin's *Caleb Williams* can all be seen as explaining why the detective, when he appeared in fiction, did so as himself a crook, or at least a shady and ambiguous character. The English, in particular, appear to have disliked their emerging constabulary. In 1821 Pierce Egan records that 'pig' was the slang term for a policeman (a usage that the *Oxford English Dictionary* in 1933 declared to be obsolete, but in 1982 had to exhibit as current again). When criminals were caught it was commonly through the agency of informers no better than themselves, and thus the prevention of crime was seen as a trade little less felonious and reprehensible than crime itself. As late as 1869 a Commissioner of Metropolitan Police could declare that detection is 'viewed with the greatest suspicion and jealousy by the majority of Englishmen and is, in fact, entirely foreign to the habits and feelings of the nation'. Above all, catching thieves, as distinct from giving orders that they be caught, is the business only of persons well down the social ladder.

Eventually the detective, alike in the public mind and in the fiction reflecting that mind, begins to turn morally respectable. But at the same time he stays put as the next thing to a low-life character. He is very much a menial, and his services can even be privately hired from his official employers by prosperous people, as are Sergeant Cuff's by Lady Verinder in Wilkie Collins's *The Moonstone*. Often, too, he is represented as something of a Dogberry, and intellectually far from up to his job. Conan Doyle accepts this convention of professional policemen being far from clever enough for the solving of the mysteries confronting them. He accepts, too, what may be called the social slant on these people. Since they are essentially lower-class they are at a disadvantage as soon as their inquiries bring them into contact or conflict with their betters. When they apply to Holmes for help it is partly because he has a mighty intellect (although not so mighty as that of his lethargic brother, Mycroft Holmes) and partly because, being a gentleman, he can tackle even a duke on equal terms if need be. This is established convention. But in one crucial regard the figure of Holmes is radically original. He is the first gentleman to get down on hands and knees in search of footprints and that famous tobacco ash.

The professionals, however, although commonly much of a muchness and rather dull fellows, can be used to liven up a narrative at times. Thus it may be recalled that Anthony Trollope, seeking to give a fillip to the middle stretch of *The Eustace Diamonds*, hits upon the police detectives Bunfit and Gager, and allows considerable scope to their harrying poor Lizzie Eustace over her missing jewels. Trollope clearly finds this a no-trouble job. Bunfit is a current reliable stereotype: a plebeian thief-catcher, tenacious, deferential, conscientiously demotic in syntax and vocabulary, whose activities are controlled from off-stage by Major Mackintosh, high up in the Police and moving in the best society. The convention continues to crop up occasionally in fiction proper whenever a little criminal investigation is required — as by Joseph Conrad, for example, in *The Secret Agent*. In detective stories it frequently takes the form either of team-work or of tug-of-war between an upper-class amateur and professional policemen assumed to be late risen from the people.

The most famous of these latter is, I suppose, Inspector Bucket in *Bleak House*, who is this stand-by of sensation fiction enriched by the genius of Dickens. For Bucket is the incarnation of that essentially lower-middle-class (rather than plebeian) respectability which his creator, a devoted student of the annals of contemporary crime, saw as having replaced the morally disreputable associations and standards of the detectives and informers of an earlier period. At the same time his heredity is evident in him. As he performs his 'cruel tasks', he 'exudes an air of kindly concern for his victims' in a manner that it is not Dickens's purpose that we should find wholly agreeable; and his attitude to the unfortunate Joe is a muddle of random benevolence and 'private dirty work' without justification in the enforcing of public order.

Finally here one has to return to Conan Doyle. As detective puzzles his stories are often elementary, and he was by no means eager to exploit the newer techniques of criminal investigation: notably the tremendous innovation of identification by fingerprints. There has, of course, been an increasing problem of verisimilitude in this region during the later phases in the development of the detective story. The average reader will not be wholly uninformed about modern criminal investigation as a highly developed and sophisticated machine, whose operatives can call for aid at will upon a number of scientific disciplines. The spectacle of so powerful an engine ticking over idly while the mighty intellect or the little grey cells do the job is not easy to render convincing. Holmes, of course, is represented (rather vaguely) as having his retort and test-tube side. But essentially — and unlike most modern private eyes — he owes his fame to the deployment of a very considerable literary art. And, in particular, much of the charm of his adventures adheres in their setting: each one is a period piece. Indeed, several periods are involved, and in his forty years of activity Holmes is deftly shown as passing from one social climate to another. The atmosphere of the Decadence, for example, hangs over his earlier exploits and habits as not over the later. (Consider that hypodermic syringe, which — unlike the violin and the tobacco jar — has to be rigorously excluded from television evocations of the Baker Street milieu.)

Conan Doyle's ambitions as a historical novelist ('ponderously fictionalized Macaulay', as one of his best critics no doubt justly says) are perhaps of significance here. His detail is always meticulously of an age, even if it be his own. And here some curious problems in the drift of public taste present themselves. In Holmes's earlier phase the reader is required to be impressed by the fact that the great detective has never heard of Thomas Carlyle, to say nothing of the earth's habit of revolving round the sun. By the end of his career Holmes has become a polymath capable of enchanting a dinner-table with authoritative pronouncements 'on miracle plays, on mediaeval pottery, on Stradivarius violins, on the Buddhism of Ceylon, and on the warships of the future — handling each as though he had made a special study of it'. Not only is Sergeant Cuff behind us. We are well on the way to Lord Peter Wimsey and his appalling transatlantic blood-brother, Philo Vance.

Novels

MY FIRST NOVEL, *Mark Lambert's Supper*, was published in 1954. Although it was generally well received, there were not lacking those who declared it to be another detective story, but a detective story dolled up in verbal garments which absurdly evoked the shade of Henry James. This was not, I think, altogether unfair, and that I could manage straight pastiche if I chose is attested to by my including in the book a letter very colourably purporting to be from the pen of James himself. But I certainly didn't intend to set myself up on the stilts of another man's style. Where I did, I think, go wrong was in supposing that, since the story turned on the career of a novelist born in the early 1850s, the narrator's voice itself should carry, in syntax and vocabulary, a certain period flavour. This was perhaps a hazy notion, but I stuck to it in the main, although not in places where there was advantage in strongly contrasting old and new. One such place, early in the book, is in the radio programme which I represent as occasioned by the centenary of the novelist Mark Lambert's birth, where the fashionably informal culture-chatter of a panel of young literary journalists is set over against the polished periods of an older man, the 'artfully-cadenced' Sir Charles Shaxby, formerly a close friend of the essentially Victorian Lambert himself.

But if I now have reservations about the style, so also do I have about my handling of the fable. To have a secret to reveal, a mystery to resolve, is a resource of fiction as old as the *Oedipus Tyrannus*. But it is a resource that requires to be deployed with continence. That improbabilities buttress one another may be true of farce, and seen to operate successfully in, say, *The Comedy of Errors*. But the principle is of narrow application. There is hazard in interdigitating even as few as two separate mysteries, and greater hazard in setting such a premium on the sustaining of suspense that the truth about each comes tumbling out (as in an efficient detective story) virtually on a final page. At the end of

Mark Lambert's Supper Lambert's 'golden decade' novels turn out to have been written by somebody else, and with this revelation there is ingeniously dovetailed the resolution of a dreadful question which has suddenly seemed to confront the two young lovers in the story: *Who was the father of Garth Dauncey?* It is, in a sense, an archetypal question, since it connects with what anthropologists have called the myth of the birth of the hero. Through the centuries innumerable works of fiction have turned on unsuspected or misconceived blood-relationships, and here is the hoary old ploy in *Mark Lambert's Supper*, coming in, pat on its cue, to complicate a dénouement already too much carpentered to suit my later taste. Indeed, the whole manner of voiding the stage, of putting the puppets back in their box, discontents me as I read. The spectacle — to put it simply — is too unlike life, the sufficient complexities of which are remote from the *olla potrida* I have been cooking up.

The theme of blood-bonds concealed or misunderstood holds for the novelist, in fact, an allure to which he does well to respond with caution: this because it belongs essentially to the field of romance rather than to that of the novel proper. And it is not in *Mark Lambert's Supper* alone that I have myself been insufficiently wary. *Avery's Mission* (1971) is far from being a romance. (Nor is it a farce, in which the theme can be treated as ludicrous.) Essentially it is a conversation comedy — if such a kind there be — and into it has to come the discovery that the strikingly clever and ruthless Italian boy, Luigi Fagandini, supposed by some to be in an improper relationship with his employer, is in fact that employer's illegitimate son, and therefore half-brother to the quintessentially English public-school boy, Avery Brenton. Again, in *Mungo's Dream* (1973), Mungo Lockhart (named by me, I suppose, out of Dunbar's 'Lament for the Makaris', but — as Mr Martin Amis remarked — in a distinguishable second-cousinship to Fielding's Tom Jones), is not, as he has been led to think, the grandson of a marquis, but the son of a dentist in very good practice. This plot has at least the merit of turning upside-down the birth of the hero myth. Finally here, there is *Andrew and Tobias* (1980), a novel in which we are almost back with the Juniper brothers in *Hare Sitting Up*. But not quite, for now my identical twins have (by an accident of war) been separated in infancy; are unaware each of the other's existence; and come together when in widely disparate conditions: Tobias will inherit the estate of his adoptive father, and Andrew has turned up there as an under-gardener. This time, the *anagnorisis* or discovery comes right at the start, and throughout the story the reunited brothers have to get along together as they may.

Of these three novels it seems to me that the first, *Avery's Mission*, comes nearest to being a success. It may be significant that it was exceptionally quickly written, but that its assured movement (which is undoubted) didn't come easily is clear from the working notes — some 6,000 words of them — which I kept as I went along. The struggle for the story, the come-and-go of the essential but sometimes only glimmering conception, is evident to me as I read through these now. Once or twice, indeed, I would seem to have lost my way entirely. Whatever can I have had in my head, I wonder, when I suggested to myself suddenly that Avery might *die* — defending his father in a riot outside La Scala in Milan? But to estimate the extreme oddity of this I am afraid it is necessary to read the book.

Rayner Heppenstall had been fond of telling me I was going to be the Scottish Proust. It was a double-barrelled joke. After all our collaborating he must have been as clear as I myself was about the twitch of my tether. But if the thought of me as a Proust was an absurdity, so was the thought of a *Scottish* Proust *per se*. Rayner was very much a Francophil; more extensively familiar with French literature than with English; and of Scots knowing nothing at all. So he may have been prejudiced. Yet there is an obvious validity, too, in the second half of the joke. A Russian Proust, even perhaps a German Proust, is dimly conceivable. But a Proust contriving for himself a cork-lined chamber in, say, Moray Place in Edinburgh is decidedly not. This conviction is of the respectable sort that one is sure of without the need of reasoning.

I suppose it is possible that, at one time or another, I had discussed with Rayner the various means of stringing novels together, of producing a 'series' or a 'sequence'. But I am rather doubtful about this. And I am confident I know just where and when the idea of *A Staircase in Surrey* came to me. It was in Cambridge very early on a summer morning.

Cambridge, and a Staircase in Surrey

IT MAY BE remembered that it was when dining with my parents in a Cambridge hotel in 1928 that I had received from Oxford a telegram from which it was possible to infer that an academic job of some sort might be the thing for me to go for. Most undergraduates, as their days of privilege dwindle, are alarmed or depressed by their own patent unemployability. Being myself quite without the resilience of Norman Cameron, who in this situation proposed as a kind of rallying cry, 'Caterpillars of the commonwealth, unite!', I had been much of this glum persuasion, and now felt that a gleam of hope had been accorded me. Prowling Cambridge on the following morning, I found I liked it very much, and I have done so ever since.

There were even two regards in which Cambridge seemed to me to have the edge on Oxford. It remained more obviously a university city, and its English Faculty seemed livelier and more up-to-date. This second point requires a little expansion. At Oxford the English School set a great deal of emphasis on the antiquities of our literature, and also on the study of the language largely in its phonological aspect: we were required to know quite a lot about how the pronunciation of one word or another changed from century to century or from region to region. Much of this made little appeal to young people of imaginative inclination, and from the inception of the Honour School down to the present day its *prima classis* is notably devoid of names that ring any bell in the field of literature. Indeed, when I last looked into the matter some years ago Aldous Huxley seemed to afford the only exception to this unfortunate state of affairs. It is true that at Oxford we were encouraged to read widely, and to write about our reading in a manner that would not gravely have offended John Dryden or Matthew Arnold. But what were called (officially, I think) the 'advanced studies' oriented themselves rather bleakly towards equipping appropriate students with the technical tools of systematic scholarship. Although learning how to handle these constituted the main road into university teaching, the wayfarers taking to it struck some of us as rather a dim crowd.

At Cambridge things seemed to be different. The prominent 'English' dons weren't at all like Percy Simpson and David Nicol Smith. There was F. R. Leavis who, although possibly a somewhat rebarbative critic, at least passionately believed in literature as existing for other purposes than to be edited with all the commas and semicolons incontestably in their right place. There was I. A. Richards, who had turned a lecture room into a kind of well-manned lab for discovering how poems are received and work, and at Magdalene College had performed a notable maieutic operation upon his prodigious pupil, William Empson. According to a kind of folklore reaching us in Oxford, Richards had handed Empson a book by Robert Graves and Laura Riding with the remark, 'There's something on page 64 that might interest you.' The book was called *A Survey of Modernist Poetry*, but what appeared on page 64 was Shakespeare's 129th sonnet — both in a modernized form and as first printed in 1609. Empson took away the book, studied the issues involved, and returned to his supervisor a week or thereabout later — having in the interim written a book of his own, which was quite soon published as *Seven Types of Ambiguity*. It is an awesomely ingenious work, and in its pages the semicolons and commas must be said to come into their own; to enter the sphere of criticism proudly and with all sails spread. For consider a line of Walter De La Mare's:

> *Beyond the rumour even of paradise, come.*

Whether we are reading this aloud or to ourselves, what the comma signals to us is a pause. But is it not necessary to pause, even if more briefly, elsewhere in the line? If we fail to *phrase* the thing, is the result not wooden and unnatural? So perhaps:

> Beyond the rumour, even of paradise, come.

Or try again:

> Beyond the rumour even, of paradise, come.

By shifting this new pause or notional comma to one or the other side of *even*, we make De La Mare bid us do different things — either 'give up even the most seductive of the rumours: the rumour of paradise', or 'give up not merely paradise itself, but even the rumour of it'. So why hasn't the poet made clear what he means? Is it possibly because — at least at some level of his mind — he sees a kind of richness in the doubt, and proposes to hand it on to us? This may stand as a simple example (too simple for Empson's book) of fascinating inquiries being pursued at Cambridge, while at Oxford we were still learning how people pronounced their vowels in Northumberland in the eleventh century, or that the late Lady Lucy Pusey, being of a conservative turn of mind, always spoke of her husband's *weskit* and *goold* watch.

The poet Dryden (mentioned above) was a Cambridge man, nurtured amid the splendours of Trinity College (to which I shall come almost at once). But having a number of occasions on which he had to produce a *Prologue to the University of Oxford*, he contrived to say in one of them:

> Oxford *to him a dearer Name shall be,*
> *Than his own Mother University.*
> Thebes *did his green unknowing Youth ingage,*
> *He chuses* Athens *in his riper age.*

This is rather displeasing, and I have no disposition to say anything of the kind in reverse, or even to compare the two places in other than a few obvious regards. It is at Cambridge that things appear to be on the larger scale. Of two colleges much of a size at their inception in Oxford and Cambridge respectively, it is the Cambridge one that is likely to have expanded the more over the centuries — ultimately, perhaps, because it is Cambridge that is set amid the richer agricultural land. Christ Church as compared with Cambridge's Trinity is a case in point. By the time Henry VIII had retrenched upon Wolsey's grandiose plans for a Cardinal College, Christ Church and Trinity (Henry's marginally later Cambridge creation) must have been much of a muchness. But although they remain twin royal foundations (with one quasi-ceremonial consequence I must now describe) it is Trinity that is much the grander concern today — and this although Christ Church, in the general Oxford view, is almost offensively grand.

The ceremonial affair was a matter of exchanged visits. About once a year, two or three Fellows of Trinity would spend a few days (or nights) with us at Christ Church, and then — perhaps at several months' remove — two or three Students of Christ Church would be entertained at Trinity. The modesty of this arrangement seemed somehow to accent its almost ambassadorial consequence, and with us there seemed to me to be a good deal of masked circumspection in the choosing of our men. I had myself been at the House for a good many years before the first occasion on which the onerous duty was imposed on me. Even then, I was sent over under the tutelage, as it were, of the most senior of my colleagues, Robin Dundas, who was eminently among those who can be relied upon never to give offence unintentionally. We did *The Times* crossword puzzle as he drove me over. I read out the clues and he supplied the answers. The day after our arrival, there was a luncheon party with ladies. It went on for a surprisingly long time, and after a brief snooze Robin took me along to the chapel of King's College to attend evensong. This — except, I suppose, when the choir school is on holiday — is (among other things, no doubt) a refined musical occasion. *O ces voix d'enfants, chantant dans le coupole!* We sat down in the nave, and presently from the chancel the voices of the invisible choristers rose, fragile and exquisite. The service was some way advanced, when I glanced at Robin and saw that he was asleep. A further snooze had stolen upon him. I was amused at this — and then a horrible thought came to me. *What if Robin began to snore?* A wild impulse to flee beset me. I was sitting next to the aisle; immediately across it there was a vacant chair; I could slip over to this without occasioning notice, and thus dissociate myself from the impending catastrophe. But a better impulse prevailed. It is not thus, I told myself, that Christ Church men should think to comport themselves one to another. So I stayed put. From beyond the choir-screen the singing, the intoning, continued; drew to a close. Not without a certain effect of impatience, the organ broke into a voluntary bidding us begone. I took a slightly bemused Robin Dundas by the elbow, gently shook it, and led him from the chapel. Ahead of us was a stately dinner at High Table and several hours in an enormous combination room.

Among a number of other Cambridge occasions I chiefly recall a second visit of this sort to Trinity. At the first the Master had been an eminent scientist, Lord Adrian, who had now been succeeded by Lord Butler — the Rab Butler whose career had taken in all the great offices of state, that of prime minister alone excepted. Having acquired the necessary grace of appearing to be seriously attentive to anybody he was conversing with, Butler was agreeable as well as impressive. The impressiveness, indeed, he shared with his surroundings. He received the visitors from Christ Church in a large drawing-room through the high windows of which, I supposed, the ferocious Richard Bentley, throughout his long Mastership, had been accustomed to hurl the epithets of rat, maggot, cabbage-head and the like at such luckless fellows of the college as traversed the court beneath. But what made this spacious chamber remarkable now was what hung on its walls: a large array of major paintings by Monet, Renoir, Cézanne, Sisley and their peers. These tremendous objects, which I found overwhelming in their unexpectedness, were not part of the general splendour of Trinity. One had to remember that Lady Butler had been a Courtauld.

I got to bed in the college late that night, but remained wakeful. So I tried repeating poetry to myself: Wordsworth's poetry, apposite to the place.

> The Evangelist St. John my Patron was,
> Three gloomy Courts are his; and in the first
> Was my abiding-place, a nook obscure!
> Right underneath, the College kitchens made
> A humming sound, less tuneable than bees,
> But hardly less industrious; with shrill notes
> Of sharp command and scolding intermix'd.
> Near me was Trinity's loquacious Clock,
> Who never let the Quarters, night or day,
> Slip by him unproclaim'd, and told the hours
> Twice over with a male and female voice.

On my first visit I had come to understand the mysterious behaviour of this clock — uncommented by Ernest de Selincourt in his edition of *The Prelude*. It strikes the hour with a series of *pongs* and then — lest it has thus awakened you or you are otherwise left in a state of uncertainty — it repeats itself with a series of *pings*. As an idea it is sensible enough, but I imagine that it may suggest an irksome officiousness to the habitually alert.

> Her pealing organ was my neighbour too;
> And, from my Bedroom, I in moonlight nights
> Could see, right opposite, a few yards off,
> The Antechapel, where the Statue stood
> Of Newton, with his Prism and silent Face.

Thus *The Prelude* as Wordsworth first composed it. Later, he added 'favouring stars' to the moonlight. I can recall having been misled by this into imagining Roubiliac's statue of the greatest of astronomers as perched on some sort of pinnacle with the stellar universe behind him. But of course it stands *within* the ante-chapel. My misconception may have been furthered by the two magical lines added to the passage by Wordsworth, probably in his sixtieth year:

> The marble index of a mind for ever
> Voyaging through strange seas of Thought, alone.

From Wordsworth's poetry I turned to prose, this time with a book before me. It was *The Masters* by C. P. Snow, the fifth in the sequence of novels about Lewis Eliot, and entirely devoted to the manoeuvres attending the election of a new head of a minor Cambridge college. To take such a book to Trinity and read it far into the small hours was, I can now see, both odd and obscurely a little lacking in fair dealing. *The Masters* is a highly competent novel. Nobody who takes it up is at all likely to abandon it before the last page. All the tangible and visible surfaces of college life are accurately there. Yet I found myself increasingly bewildered as I got further into it. Charles Snow had been a fellow of Christ's College for twenty years. Surely he must *know*? Yet his dons were as unfamiliar to me as would have been a congeries of Hottentots in their jungle. (The book is about dons only. Undergraduates scurry round once or twice, but none of them utters.) Was my sense of something alien in these characters due to their being, as it were, refugees from an environment unknown to me, called by Snow himself the corridors of power? Translated to a small and somewhat isolated self-governing and self-perpetuating corporation at a period of crisis in its affairs, they might well exhibit anxieties and obsessions, an alertness to mine and counter-mine, uncharacteristic of more authentic academic persons. But was there not (I asked myself as I closed the book, and before I did go to sleep) an odd sort of complacence spread over the presented spectacle, almost an assumption of edification as inherent in it?

I woke up the following morning with a feeling that I had perhaps been unjust to C. P. Snow's novel. I had myself, it was true, spent many years (and was to spend a good many more) on the governing body of an Oxford college without running into either men or manoeuvres such as he described. But his scene was, in a sense, validated in what was plainly a source of his novel: the *Memoirs* of Mark Pattison, published in 1885. So perhaps *The Masters* had to be seen as a serious attempt to portray a body of scholars coping with a curiously insulated and rarely recurring crisis in its affairs.

Only, was *The Masters* perhaps (in a narrow sense) *too* serious, pervasively without thought to make a moment merry? It is in comedy, I told myself — comedy rather than tragedy — that there lies man's least ineffective retort upon the void, and comedy ought not lightly to be discarded from representative fiction. If I ever came to write a novel, or series of novels, centred on the way of life most familiar to me, the spirit of comedy should declare itself, however inadequately, on the opening page; should quicken to life even in dark places.

And this was, in fact, a seminal moment with me. It was a few years after that second visit to Trinity College in Cambridge that I began to write *The Gaudy*, the first of five books called collectively *A Staircase in Surrey*. *The Gaudy* was published in 1974, and the final volume, *Full Term*, four years later. With the possible exception of my volume in the *Oxford History of English Literature*, this quintet represents my most sustained single effort as a writer. But both under my own name and as Michael Innes I have produced a good deal of fiction in the succeeding decade. Innes has been content more or less to hold his own. Stewart has here and there attempted to explore a little further such abilities as have been granted him, particularly in the writing of simple short stories. 'Sweets from a Stranger', which occupies the final few pages of *Parlour 4 and other stories* published in 1986, is my favourite, and by way of Epilogue I reproduce it here.

SWEETS FROM A STRANGER

IF I WERE a professional writer I could probably make a short story — a modishly sinister short story — out of the mere episode (as it was) that I propose to recount here. Alternatively, and were I a historian, I could so frame it that it showed like a footnote to a phase of Scottish social history. Indeed, with something like this latter I see I had better begin.

In the final quarter of the eighteenth century, then, the superior classes in Edinburgh began building themselves a New Town. Hitherto they had lived in a more or less mediaeval city to the south of the Nor' Loch, higgledy-piggledy with the poorest of the poor, but fortified, no doubt, by an equal contiguity with such elements of the Scottish aristocracy as maintined a town house in the capital. In many instances the migrating *haute bourgeoisie*, while losing the contiguity, very consciously maintained shades and degrees of kinship with this augustly territorial stratum of Scottish society. This is a very Scottish thing.

When they had built their New Town the *haute bourgeoisie* fairly quickly decided that it ought to contain a New School to which to send their sons. Hitherto these sons, had, of course, also lived higgledy-piggledy with the sons of the humble and unwashed, and if they sorted themselves out from time to time it was to engage in 'bickers' with their less fortunate fellows. A 'bicker' was a gang-fight likely to lead to a good deal in the way of bruises and gashes occasioned by clubs and stones. I don't think that as a boy I had so much as heard of these broils, which had evaporated from the popular memory. Perhaps I first read of them in Lockhart's *Life* of Walter Scott.

Hitherto, again, gentle and simple had gone to school together. The Edinburgh High School had for centuries held an unchallenged place at the head of Scottish scholastic education. Everybody went there, down to the future Sir Walter himself. But it was tough and rough. Moreover, it was situated, not in the commanding position it enjoys today, but in what was now thought of simply as the slums. The persons planning or plotting for a new and exclusive school made much of the inconvenience — and worse — likely to be encountered by their sons in their daily going to and fro this ancient place of education. So the new school was built, and Sir Walter was wheeled in to make an opening speech.

I have written all this by way of highlighting the essentially insulating class-structure of society which intensified itself (I believe) throughout the nineteenth century — perhaps even more in England than in Scotland — and into which were born those who, like myself, passed their infancy before the First World War.

In due course I was despatched to the preparatory department of the 'new' school — now, indeed, within sight of its centenary. I don't think there were many — if, indeed, any — boarders in the prep, and I certainly cannot yet have come to think of the boarding houses as strongholds of mysterious wickedness. I knew nothing about wickedness, except as something that frequently turned up in the Bible. And from the Bible when produced I had early formed the covert habit of removing my mind and thinking of Tom Thumb. My mother, however, must have been very aware of the Devil, and that he was among us, having great wrath. For on one of the first days of my returning from school she suddenly gripped my arm in its bright new blue blazer and uttered a strange question with yet stranger intensity.

'Donald, you *do* know that there is such a thing as *vice* in this world?'

Here again was something on which my mind was entirely blank. But I had discovered by this time how best to cope with sudden incomprehensibilities from grown-ups, and I hastened to assure my mother that there was nothing I didn't know about vice. This, perhaps a shade oddly, at once relaxed whatever anxiety had been harbouring in her consciousness. But what can it have been? The question puzzles me to this day. What scope can she have imagined the Devil as having for manoeuvre in what was called Class IB? In IB we weren't exactly toddlers any longer, but our ages must have averaged out at about eight. It wasn't as if my mother bore any sort of habitually prurient mind. In her own way, she belonged to an Age of Innocence as completely as I did myself.

And here is another type of insulation operative in this environment in which I grew up. There was a kind of tacit censorship upon any explicit ventilation of the seamier side of things. So far as I can remember, almost nothing of the sort even got into our newspapers. The existence of mere poverty was, of course, acknowledged; and although I don't recall hearing that distinction between the 'poor' and the 'good poor' which many Victorian philanthropists had managed to be aware of, there was, I believe, a vague and diffused feeling that a condition of indigence was in itself reprehensible, and that contact with it should, if unobtrusively, be avoided. Cousins of my own age in Moray in the distant North, some of them of families a good deal grander than ours, I had observed on holidays playing freely with the farm labourers' children. Nothing of the sort with us. All Edinburgh boys other than our own schoolfellows we referred to as keelies, which is Scots for street-arabs. And for weeks on end, any member of the poor with whom I ever conversed was in uniform, like tram conductors or our own maids — the latter being distinctively dressed in crisp aprons and caps, and being rather carefully 'well-spoken' as well. It would only be when a tramp (and there were a good many tramps around) came to the door and had to be found a 'piece' that I held the slightest commerce with these virtual non-persons.

I appear rather to be harping on all this. But it serves in part to explain the element of shock in my small adventure.

'Adventure', I see, is the wrong word. 'Experience' might be better. But, whatever it was, it was something startlingly new to me, and I am surprised to find that I cannot with any certainty put a date to it. In formal studies of the psychology of childhood, precise dating must, I imagine, be vital — and by 'dating' I of course mean determining and stating the age in years and months at which one or another significant act of behaviour has been produced. Even when children crop up in works of fiction one rather wants to know just how old they are supposed to be. When a novelist hedges over this, ignoring the point, or passing over it emphatically and with no reiteration, I am left with the sense of him as not confident that he knows quite what happens to children when. This may be unjust, and I am far from being an authority on literary matters. (In point of fact I work as a solicitor — of the kind called in Scotland, perhaps a shade mysteriously, Writers to the Signet.)

But I return to my episode (another possible word for the thing) and its dubious chronology. And here I am at least given a hint by my bicycle. The bicycle comes into the story because one of the first explanations I afforded myself of what was happening was simply that there was a design to purloin it. And it was my *second* bicycle. I am very certain of that. My first bicycle had been an unassuming and locally manufactured affair. My second was resplendent: rigid, rapid, and reliable. And my father, since he was a leading surgeon, distinctly well-off, and amiably disposed to spoil his family, may well have given it to me on my tenth birthday. Further than this on the point, I can't go.

I was already not very fond of games, and I wasn't much of a reader either, although I have become something of one since. In summer I collected butterflies, and in winter postage stamps: clearly I wasn't an imaginative boy. I may also have been slightly isolated from my schoolfellows — this because we lived not in the New Town strictly regarded (the 'windy parallelograms', as somebody or other has called those august Georgian squares and oblongs) but in a large and somewhat retired house on its western fringe. This controlled the route I took home on my bicycle. If my journey was straight from the school itself I was companioned for part of the way up the ascent that led eventually to Princes Street. But if it was from our playing-fields, which lay at some remove from the main buildings and boarding-houses, I was on my own from the start, and quite early on there was one very steep incline which could be negotiated only by dismounting and pushing the Raleigh uphill.

In Edinburgh many people live in tenements. Elsewhere, these might be called apartment blocks, or flats, or even mansions. But here they distinguishably exhibit something of their ancestry in the dwellings of the Old Town. Four or five storeys high, and with their ground floor occasionally turned into shops, they may extend the full length of a street as an uninterrupted terrace, with at regular intervals common staircases, stony and often smelly as well, giving access to small dwelling-places on either hand. Occasionally, however, these dwelling-places turn out to be, through some mysterious agency, more commodious than one would expect, and to be inhabited by persons distinctly of more consequence than their neighbours, and who don't at all seem to mind the often exhausting, grimy, and malodorous approach to their hall door. There is in this — as I say — some shadow of ancient times, when, on what has come to be called the 'Royal Mile', men powerful in the land were contented to live up just such a staircase, among neighbours who were at the best of the mechanic class.

Here and there around the city and its environs are oddly sited small examples of this sort of thing. It is as if volcanic eruption had tossed these bits and pieces high into the clouds, and then landed them at random, topside up but sadly in disrepair, in one unexpected place or another. There was a particularly good example on my left hand as I shoved my bicycle up that hill, and I believe that for some time I hadn't liked the look of it. But just what the look was, I can no longer say. The old woman and her gesture are etched on my brain, but the decrepit and — surely — half-abandoned building (demolished many years ago) largely eludes me. I have a vague picture of three storeys, the uppermost having windows broken for the most part and with rags of curtains blowing through. And I see the frontage rising not straight from the pavement, as was commonly so with tenements, but beyond a small patch of garden thick with thistle and nettle. The old woman as she makes that gesture is knee-high among this — which means that she has advanced a foot or two from the open door of the building.

She had beckoned me. She was not only old, but haggard and dirty and bedraggled and dressed in what I thought of as rags as well. I was instantly horrified and frightened: of that I am certain. But the situation lasted only for a moment. I had shoved on the handlebars with a will, and the thing was behind me.

By the time I arrived home — and it was nearly all a breezy coasting once I reached the top of the hill — I knew I was going to be mum about that weird soliciting. Provisionally, I had decided that the old woman was a witch. I knew about witches not through fairy-stories or the like, but as a matter of family tradition. My maternal grandfather, having retired from the Indian Civil Service, had occupied himself in farming some scraps of land rented from a kinsman on high ground about midway between the small Scottish towns of Nairn and Forres. Much of the surrounding countryside is now patched with large plantations, collectively dignified with the title of Darnaway Forest. At a former time it may well have been heath — and blasted heath at that. Certainly from the upper windows of my grandfather's house one could remark a ruin, perhaps a couple of miles away, traditionally known as Darnaway Castle, and not far from this a small tump called Macbeth's Hillock. My mother, stretching (or contracting) things a little, would assert that it was on her father's ground that the new Thane of Cawdor encountered the Weird Sisters. It was almost as if we had witches in the family.

I knew that witches went in for that mysterious 'wickedness', and it must have been this that put it in my head that the old woman beckoning from her doorway was proposing to lure me from my bicycle (perhaps with the offer of a poke of jujubes) in order that it should instantly be carried off by a confederate. This persuasion remained with me as I hurried away, curiously shaken.

The incident repeated itself two afternoons later, and again I ignored that disturbing summons. But this time there was a new element in the situation — or, rather, there was something new obscurely surfacing in myself. And now I hesitate, since here are fugitive sensations fished up after more than fifty years. Am I dramatizing them if I suggest that a kind of dark excitement was getting hold of me? Certainly I no longer felt that it would be my bicycle that might be at risk if I obeyed that beckoning finger — the very gesture (my later self imagines) with which Goethe's Mephistopheles utters to Faust his final dire command: *Her zu mir!* The temptation — for it certainly now had that dimension — was alive in me. Prudent teachers, apprehensive parents are aware of such dark possibilities when they counsel children never to accept sweets from strangers. Still, I once more got safely home.

Some days went by, and again there was a 'practice'. (It was the term in which we played rugger.) As I 'changed' after the game and knotted my football-boots round my neck and wheeled out my bicycle, I knew that I ought to take the longer route home. But I didn't.

And there, yet again, she was: the filthy old hag — and not a soul else in sight. This time, however, she not only beckoned to me. She called out as well. In a cracked, wheedling voice she called out from before that shabby doorway:

'Maister, sweet wee maister, will ye no come ben?'

Donald, you do know that there is such a thing as vice *in this world?*

My mother's former words may, or may not, have been in my ears. I can't in the least tell. But I think I almost felt I knew, despite my innocence, what the reader (who isn't innocent) feels he knows: that some small, squalid, yet essentially evil thing confronted me were I to take a single forward step. But I took it. I wanted to *know*. Perhaps it was just that.

Here I must return for a moment to the theme of that insulated society within which I was growing up. I had heard my father speak of something he called 'the submerged tenth', and of an outrageous person named Lloyd George, who had made some minatory reference to 'the masses far down below'. But I had never glimpsed the inside of even a normal working-class dwelling, let alone of a slum interior of any sort. Occasionally I had been sent with a message to our jobbing gardener, and delivered it on the doorstep of what could be termed, I suppose, his hovel. But conscious that this could afford me a direct view of what must be its only living-room, I would keep my eyes as I spoke firmly directed on my own shoes. If at a pantomime or a play there was a scene set in what purported to be a cottage room, it would in fact be something like thirty feet from back to front and side to side. Television, which now renders the most nicely brought up children comfortably familiar with squalor in confined spaces and jostlings before a kitchen sink, still lay in the future. And now three forward steps had taken me into a totally alien world.

In front of me was a dusty stone staircase, protected by wooden banisters and a handrail of which only fragments remained. On my right was a door roughly boarded up — perhaps to discourage homeless persons from seeking shelter for the night in whatever small and abandoned dwelling-spaces lay beyond. On my left, but open, was the door of the still-beckoning old woman's own domain. Retreat remained perfectly possible to me, but I was as incapable of turning back as a mouse lured into a trap by a whiff of cheese. The room I thus found myself in wasn't, in fact, minute, but appeared so because everywhere encumbered with the forlorn detritus of utterly disordered living. It seemed that wherever I looked there was some broken or tattered object that ought to have been thrown away: a rusty mangle, pans without handles and pots without lids, piles of rags. The least battered piece of furniture was a bed, but even this was propped up at one corner on a wooden box. There was a horsehair mattress on it, with a triangular tear in its soiled covering so that the stuff showed through, and with a couple of tumbled blankets at its foot. I had never seen a bed on which it was impossible to imagine sheets, and as I looked at this one I suddenly felt very sick. Managing to avert my gaze, I saw that the room had a single window, facing the road and kerb on which my bicycle was presumably still leaning. Before the window was a chair, which seemed somehow to be perched on wheels. And on the chair sat a boy of about my own age.

For a moment I thought him much older, and then I saw that this appearance resulted from his features' being pinched and drawn. I saw, too, that he was awkwardly slumped in his chair, so that his body in its almost ragged clothing showed like a partly emptied sack. And he was powerless to right or relieve this posture in any way. I had heard of paralysis. This was it.

The old woman had taken me by the arm, as if to lead me, all-reluctant, up to the invalid. But now, seeing his discomfort, she let go. Almost, she had forgotten me.

'Jamie, ween,' she said as she hurried to him, 'I'll gie ye a lift.' And in a moment she was struggling with the almost inert weight of the boy.

With difficulty, he raised both arms a little, and stroked the old woman's grimy face. I saw with amazement that his hands, at least, were still wholly within his command; that it was with deft and tender fingers that he was conveying devotion, love.

'Gran,' he said. 'Gran.'

'I've brocht ye a veesitor, Jamie,' she said. 'A laddie o' the same age as yoursel'.' And she turned to me, and in an imploring whisper that would have moved a tougher child than I asked: 'Ye'll bide a wee, young maister? He's that lonesome, my Jamie — and whiles he sees a laddie wi' legs to him gang by.'

'Yes,' I said awkwardly. And I brought myself to come close to Jamie and kneel beside him.

Again with difficulty, Jamie raised his arms, and with the same deft tenderness I had just witnessed he stroked the football boots hanging from my neck.

'Ye play foot-ba'?' he asked.

'Yes, I've been playing this afternoon, Jamie.' I was about to add that I was no good at the game, and didn't much care for it. But I realized in time that this would be the wrong thing to say, and fell silent.

'D'ye pick up the ba and rin wi' it?'

'Yes — it's that sort of football.'

'It's an unco queer way wi' a foot-ba.' Jamie laughed softly. 'But ane way or anither, I'd like fine to play foot-ba.'

'Perhaps you will one day, Jamie. When you're better, you will.'

After that, conversation was difficult. But I kept it up for a time, chiefly conscious of shame at the nebulous and mysterious and nasty fears that I had nursed about Jamie's grandmother. Then I felt it was time to go. Had I known beforehand what I was to encounter — I told myself —I would have brought Jamie a present. As it was, I had nothing. Or almost nothing. I felt in the pocket of my shorts, and what my hand came on was a coin. I brought it out. It was a shilling. My intention betrayed itself before I knew its ghastly inadequacy, inappropriateness. What my father called a 'tip' would be utterly wrong. I glanced at the shilling, and suddenly felt a vast relief. On the face of it was not George V, but Queen Victoria. The thing was as good as an antique.

'Jamie,' I said, 'take this. Please take this. It's very old. It would do in a collection. Like a medal.'

Back home, I tumbled it all out. My mother was apprehensive lest I had 'caught' something. By my father was very angry. I supposed he was furious with me for having entered such a house; furious with Jamie's grandmother for having wheedled me into it. But it wasn't at all like that.

'It's appalling!' my father thundered. 'It's a disgrace to the medical and sanitary service of the city.' ('Social services' had not then been thought of.) 'A senile old woman and a helpless child unregarded in such conditions! Paraplegia, as the popular expression has it. Muscular dystrophy, quite plainly. I'll have it out with them! With that damned Town Clerk, or with the Lord Provost himself! Your Jamie and his grandmother will be properly looked after, Donald. That I promise you.'

And so it came about. My father was proud of being an Edinburgh man. *Nisi Dominus frustra*, our civic motto said. Except the Lord keep the City, they labour in vain that build it. The conditions I encountered ought to be held intolerable in any Christian community. My father's indignation and standing were irresistible. Jamie's grandmother was removed to what is now called an Old Folk's Home, and Jamie to some sort of orphanage. I don't suppose that either of them, thus sundered, survived for long.

Index

Index